THE MINIMUM COST OF LIVING

THE MACMILLAN COMPANY
NEW YORK · BOSTON · CHICAGO · DALLAS
ATLANTA · SAN FRANCISCO

MACMILLAN & CO., LIMITED
LONDON · BOMBAY · CALCUTTA
MELBOURNE

THE MACMILLAN CO. OF CANADA, LTD.
TORONTO

THE MINIMUM COST OF LIVING

A STUDY OF FAMILIES OF LIMITED INCOME IN NEW YORK CITY

BY

WINIFRED STUART GIBBS

SUPERVISOR HOME ECONOMICS, NEW YORK ASSOCIATION FOR IMPROVING THE CONDITION OF THE POOR, LECTURER IN HOUSEHOLD ARTS, TEACHERS COLLEGE, COLUMBIA UNIVERSITY, AUTHOR OF "ECONOMICAL COOKING," "FOOD FOR THE INVALID AND CONVALESCENT,"—ETC., ETC.

New York
THE MACMILLAN COMPANY
1917

Set up and electrotyped. Published March, 1917.

INTRODUCTION

One of the chief aims of an organization like the Association for Improving the Condition of the Poor is to help others to help themselves. It is frequently more helpful to teach a given family how its income can be made to more nearly meet its needs than to supplement their income with relief. This is always the case if their income is sufficient when wisely used to meet their actual necessities although it may not be sufficient even for them unless used wisely with much planning. Perhaps one of the most essential factors in thrift in family expenditures is careful planning. Careful planning inevitably means a systematic record of expenditures. Making this record in itself is of the greatest use in developing thrift and lays a firm foundation for profiting from errors in thrift—from hasty poor judgments in expenditures. No corrective is more effective than a record of an unwise expenditure.

It was with these thoughts in mind that the

Association for Improving the Condition of the Poor developed some two years ago a simple but practical family budget book for the use of families known to the Association over continuous periods of time, that is, families in which the dependency either because of widowhood or of chronic sickness was relatively long continued, usually ending only with the coming to working age of children in these families. The use of this systematic method of recording family expenditures has been most beneficial. An interesting thing about it is the interest which these families themselves take, somewhat contrary to expectation, in keeping the record. Incidentally, much useful information has been collected as to the food habits of families of moderate incomes in New York City. It has seemed worth while to present in some detail the results of this systematic record of family expenditures in a typical group of families and to interpret these in the light of what it is reasonable to hope can still be accomplished in the direction of education of such families to further increase the usefulness of their income in terms of better food, better clothing and better housing. The assembling of this information has been made by Miss

Winifred S. Gibbs who has for the past ten years been in charge of the Division of Home Economics.

(Signed) Bailey B. Burritt,
General Director, New York
Association for Improving
the Condition of the Poor.

TABLE OF CONTENTS

PART I

THE STUDY AS A WHOLE

CHAPTER I

CHAPTER II

PART II

EXPENSE ACCOUNTS OF THE SEVENTY-FIVE FAMILIES

PART III

WHAT THE STUDY REVEALED

CHAPTER I

CHAPTER II

CHAPTER III

CHAPTER IV

CHAPTER V

CHAPTER VI

FOREWORD

In 1906, the Dean of a technical college said to the writer, "I can find plenty of girls who realize the value of Household Art courses in school, and plenty who teach these courses well. What I want now is someone on the firing line who will show my students how to connect their classroom work with the real questions of the day."

The women who did the work on which the present study is based are all on the "firing line." The work was begun ten years ago by the New York Association for Improving the Condition of the Poor. The first purpose was to give simple lessons in diet and cooking to the mothers of underfed children. These families were all under the care of the Association. It was soon found, however, that in order to do any constructive work and really help the families, the food problem could not be considered independently. As the work developed the family budget as a whole came to be the foundation for all instruction. The dietitian based her diet and cooking lessons on the food budget; the sewing teacher based hers on the clothing item. The family budgets dealt with in the following pages were, of necessity, on a minimum basis. The word minimum is used to denote certain results of work done. This work included observation of results for the purpose of determining the lowest sum on which the families could maintain health and working power. This was for the purpose of making best use of the money in hand, and never for the purpose of keeping the families on a low standard. The families were those of widows, who, by reason of the death of the wage earner, had been granted a definite monthly cash allowance. This allowance was based on a carefully planned estimate of needs. Furthermore, the Association hoped by the fixing of such an estimate, and by a record of its working out to be of direct service to other families whose incomes were practically the same as that allowed these families. The results of this experiment are set forth in the following pages. Because of the lack of margin it was necessary to give careful attention to each item so that no one should rob the other.

The workers have endeavored to present a piece

of work in which the human element should be brought out, but one in which this element should be related definitely to a sound scientific background. Direct good to the families has been the chief aim. It is hoped, however, that the results of this instruction can be so formulated as to be of service to all who are concerned in our present day industrial and social problem.

The following field workers have made this study possible:—Mrs. Emma Carter Schultz, Miss Marion Mudge, Miss J. B. F. Parramore, Dr. Bertha F. Johnson, Miss Elisabeth Banks, Miss Margaret Schmidt, Miss Elizabeth Guilford, and Miss Bessie G. Chamberlayne. They have contributed unstinted personal service with the families and enthusiastic professional coöperation in the division.

The writer extends grateful acknowledgments to Professor Henry C. Sherman and Professor Robert E. Chaddock of Columbia University and to Dr. C. F. Langworthy, Department of Agriculture, Washington, D. C., for helpful criticisms and suggestions.

W. S. G.

PART I

THE STUDY AS A WHOLE

THE MINIMUM COST OF LIVING

A STUDY OF FAMILIES OF LIMITED INCOME IN NEW YORK CITY

CHAPTER I

OBJECT OF THE STUDY

FROM Sir William Petty in 1672 to Dr. Robert Coit Chapin in 1906, each study of the family budget has made its own contribution to the sum of human well-being. The earlier workers undertook these studies primarily that the resulting data might be used to improve social conditions. Their viewpoint was the broadly social, and contact with individual families ceased when the families had contributed the necessary information. Furthermore, much of the field work was done by those whose interest ended when the actual gathering of data was completed.

The present study was also begun in the hope of making a contribution that might help to improve social conditions. The immediate plan, however, was to so far improve family groups that they might become stronger units in the future. Those in charge of the work had a decided advantage over their predecessors in that their field workers were women specially fitted by training and interests for the doing of such work.

Expense accounts were collected from one hundred and fifty families, but in order to make the study concise seventy-five were chosen for presentation. These seventy-five families are typical of the income groups represented in this study.

Briefly, the families reported upon fall into the following groups according to size:

3	families—widow	and	two	children
26	"	"	" three	"
19	"	"	" four	"
15	"	"	" five	"
5	"	"	" six	"
6	"	"	" seven	"
1	family	"	" eight	"

According to nationality they form the following groups:

American	19	Irish	28
English	1	Scandinavian	2
German	17	Austrian	1
Italian	5	Bohemian	2

The function of the Home Economics work of the Association is fundamentally educational. Its aim is to establish each family on the basis of a self-sustaining unit. Therefore, the results of the present study are presented as nearly as possible from the standpoint of the normal.

METHOD EMPLOYED IN MAKING THE STUDY

For the first few years budgets were kept in a very informal way, but in each case they were used as a basis for the lessons planned. In 1914 systematic budget keeping was begun in the families of more or less fixed income. By means of these expense books the women have learned to view their home problems as a whole. They have been trained to accurate thinking and to accurate expression. They have learned habits of thrift from the mere record on paper of their expenditure. Finally, they have had the advantage of comparing the records and results of bad dietary habits with good, and have learned in the same way to reorganize their expenditures for the other items of the budget.

The Association cares nothing for tables of statistics that stop at tabulation. The tabulations must point backward to some good accomplished and onward to possible increased good in the future. Dr. Chapin has said that in compiling results of such work: "Both the intensive and the extensive methods are valuable and should supplement each other. With the extensive method to give breadth and perspective, and the intensive study to give color and definiteness to the outlines obtained by the extensive method, the study of the family budget can best be made to bring out 'the standard of living.'"

In formulating a plan of work, in each family the workers collected information and made plans somewhat as follows:

Summary of the economic situation in each family:

- Instruction in budget making,
- Instruction in carrying out the budget planned,
- Plan of dietary needed by individual family,
- Plan of clothing needs,
- Lessons in cooking,
- Lessons in sewing.

The first step in getting this information was to hold a friendly conference with the housekeeper. Few of the women were accustomed to "taking account of stock." A clear statement of the family resources was followed by careful instruction as to how best to divide the income. One point should be emphasized—the women were to a large extent given freedom of choice, the expense accounts being controlled only by advice.

Someone has called a budget a "financial prophecy." The women in the present group were taught that to make a budget meant to forecast a future of improved health and freedom from the wear and tear of a hand-to-mouth existence. The word "food" came to stand for something besides the unpaid grocery bill. "Clothing" began to fulfill its chief mission—that of helping to conserve the family self-respect and happiness. In short, the housekeepers learned to adjust their expenditures so that the account books were genuine human documents.

The advance from their customary slipshod methods to systematic adjustment was not made in a day. Slowly and patiently housekeeper and teacher worked together. The progress was slow but the results satisfactory. One of the women had never learned simple addition. In her zeal to have a satisfactory expense book she taught herself to add. Her method at first was to group all the figures of the same denomination together, make separate additions of each group and then to arrive at the grand total by a process equally intricate.

The women were taught to care for the children's food needs first. It was not always easy to convince them of the necessity for this, since busy, tired mothers were apt to say—"The children must take just what we do." Instruction therefore included planning of a dietary which would fill the children's needs and satisfy the adults' tastes without undue elaboration of cooking processes.

From the beginning the teachers realized that the clothing budget must be very carefully planned. Necessarily the sum fixed was somewhat meagre. It was felt, however, that a carefully administered clothing allowance would do much to increase the general morale of the family. As in the case of food a slipping to a low standard in matters of dress came almost invariably from fatigue, ill health and the resulting loss of desire and power to think and plan. The direct influence of neat and suitable clothing can hardly be overestimated. It is perhaps in this item that the lack of margin in the budget was most keenly felt. Practically all of the families, however, were recipients of gifts of clothing from friends and relatives at various times throughout the year, which served somewhat to supplement the amount allowed for this item. As is the case with most mothers, nearly all of these women sacrificed their own tastes and comfort in clothing so that the children might be neatly and attractively dressed.

These lessons were used as one of the means to the end of family upbuilding. The cooking lessons were planned with the food item in the budget as a basis. The sewing lessons bore a similar relation to the clothing item.

Before the granting of the cash allowance expense accounts were simply records of daily purchases. When the form was made up for the present expense books experience of former years was the chief deciding factor. It was felt that the budget page must do more than afford a place for record of expenses. This page in order to be of the greatest use must show an analysis of purchases, so that the dietitians could see at a glance whether the family was having too much or too little of any

FORM OF BUDGET SHEET

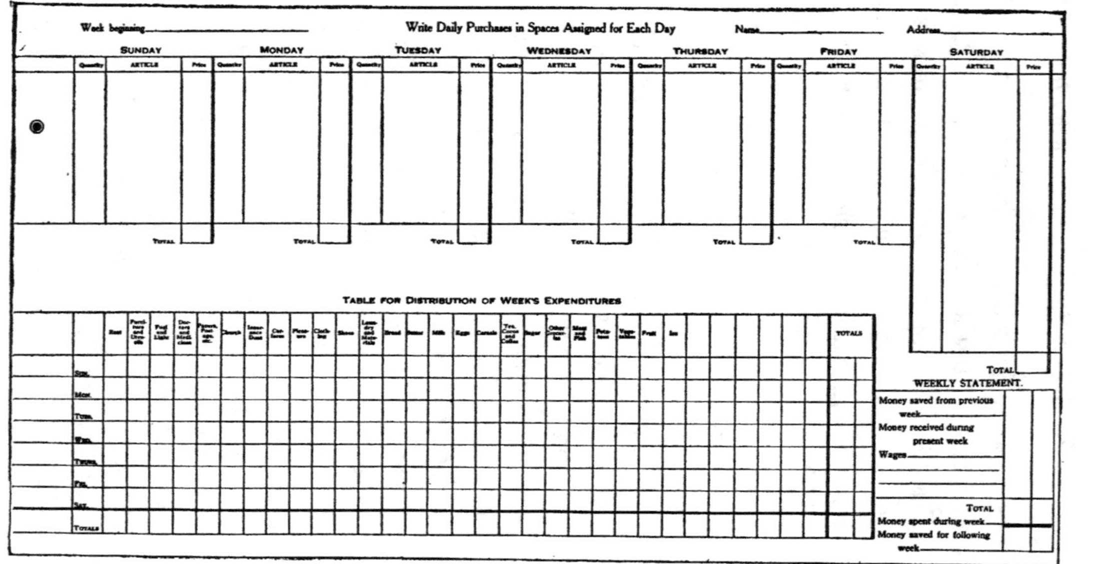

Week beginning________ Write Daily Purchases in Spaces Assigned for Each Day Name________ Address________

	SUNDAY			MONDAY			TUESDAY			WEDNESDAY			THURSDAY			FRIDAY			SATURDAY		
	Quantity	ARTICLE	Price	Quantity	ARTICLE	Price	Quantity	ARTICLE	Price	Quantity	ARTICLE	Price	Quantity	ARTICLE	Price	Quantity	ARTICLE	Price	Quantity	ARTICLE	Price
		TOTAL			TOTAL			TOTAL			TOTAL			TOTAL			TOTAL			TOTAL	

TABLE FOR DISTRIBUTION OF WEEK'S EXPENDITURES

		Rent	Furniture and Utensils	Fuel and Light	Doctors and Medicines	Papers, Postage, etc.	Church	Insurance Dues	Car-fares	Pleasure	Clothing	Shoes	Laundry and Materials	Bread	Butter	Milk	Eggs	Cereals	Tea, Cocoa and Coffee	Sugar	Other Groceries	Meat and Fish	Potatoes	Vegetables	Fruit	Ice							TOTALS
	Sun.																																
	Mon.																																
	Tues.																																
	Wed.																																
	Thurs.																																
	Fri.																																
	Sat.																																
	Totals																																

WEEKLY STATEMENT.

Money saved from previous week______		
Money received during present week		
Wages______		
______		
______		
TOTAL		
Money spent during week______		
Money saved for following week______		

FORM OF RECORD KEPT BY TEACHER

NAME

ADDRESS

INDEX	Estimate of Needs	Jan	Feb.	Mar.	Apr.	May	June	July	Aug.	Sept.	Oct.	Nov.	Dec.	Special Needs of Family
Rent														
Food														
Fuel & Light														
Clothing														
Insurance														
Carfares														
Sundries														
Total														
Income														
Total														

	Bread	Butter	Milk	Eggs	Cereal	Tea Coffee Cocoa	Sugar	Meat and Fish	Potatoes	Veg.	Fruit	Lessons	Summary
Needs													
Jan.													
Feb.													
March													
April													
May													
June													
July													
Aug.													
Sept.													
Oct.													
Nov.													
Dec.													

one food. The sewing teacher must be able to decide as to whether the clothing allowance was being wisely spent. Inevitably such a page must require much detail work. The accompanying form has been in successful use for two years. The housekeepers have a separate set of loose leaves fastened together with brown paper covers for each month. This provides an easy way for checking the transfer of the surplus or deficit as the case may be, to the book for the following month.

The aim was to draw up a form of record that would show just what were the needs in each family from a home economics standpoint, what instruction was given and what were the results. The present sheet is now in use in many homes, and gives a satisfactory picture of each family for the year. The rise or fall of the dietary from month to month, the fluctuations of the income and the record of instruction give data that is valuable far beyond the limits of the home in which it is gathered.

CHAPTER II

The Estimate of Minimum Requirement

Obviously such an estimate was necessary by way of beginning, but it was equally true that the workers must keep an open mind towards the weaknesses as they developed in their own estimates. Furthermore, they must strive for flexibility so that these standards might prove guides rather than hampering boundaries.

In this preliminary discussion only the main consideration governing the estimate will be set forth. The theoretical "ideal division" of the economists is of value only as a starting point, since it is not practical to follow it in detail.

Ideal Division

Income	*Rent*	*Food*	*Operating Expenses*	*Clothing*	*"Higher Life"*
$800–1000	20% or $160 to $200	30% or $240 to $300	10% or $85 to $100	15% or $120 to $150	25% or $200 to $250

With the above estimate in mind it may be of interest to trace the actual possibilities of an income of $800 to $1000 in New York City.

PRACTICAL DIVISION

Income	*Rent*	*Food*	*Operating Expenses*	*Clothing*	*Education Recreation & Sundries*	*Saving*
$800–1000	average $150	$290–390	$39.00 fuel & light 48.00 sundries 12.00 insurance 93.00 carfare & lunches $192.00 total	$120–190	$48–78	Nothing, left when sundries and emergencies have been provided for.

Providing the breadwinner worked continuously this would leave slender provision for the innumerable unexpected needs that arise in every household, not to mention recreation and savings. As a matter of fact, every working year has many grievous breaks. Illness and strikes and holidays and "slack times" are a few of the factors to be reckoned with.

Fortunately those who live in Greater New York have the opportunity for much healthful recreation at little or no cost.

We hear much of "living standards"—but the vital spark of such a standard cannot be expressed in figures. One must be in contact with the daily lives of the families in order to appreciate the advance from discouragement to ambition. Only in this way can the figures express the good which has actually come to the homes.

The chief items in the estimate will now be considered in detail.

Shelter

Housing conditions in the poorer districts of New York City are characterized by a dreary sameness. On into the miles run streets of sordid tenements. Each of these tenements looks much like its neighbors, the chief difference being that one house may have three stories and another four; one may open into a court at the side, while still another may boast, "All light rooms." This question of shelter had been largely settled by the families themselves before the study began. It was understood that they had decided this question by securing the home neighborhood for the maximum of—shall we say negative comfort?—to be had for the amount within their means.

The rent item was estimated at $12.00 monthly for an "average family" of five. This gave fairly comfortable quarters and allowed "1½ persons to a room."

Food

The ration allowance used in this study was the standard one worked out for A. I. C. P. families.

In standardizing this allowance it was necessary to consider a large group of families, and to so express the results as to give figures that could be used by staff members outside the Home Economics Division. Obviously it was not practical to formulate a dietary every detail of which could be followed. Therefore, the ration allowance was based on the accepted dietary standards of Professor Atwater, estimating the needs of the various members of each family according to the age factors proposed by Atwater and used by the Department of Agriculture.

The table of units for making up food needs in each family is as follows:

TABLE OF UNITS

Man (17 years and over)	1.
Woman (16 years and over)	.8
Boy 16 years	.9
" 12 years–13 years, inclusive	.8
" 10 " –11 " "	.6
Girl 14 " –15 " "	.7
" 10 " –13 " "	.6
Child 6 " – 9 " "	.5
" 2 " – 5 " "	.4
" under 2 years	.3

Professor Atwater's calculations were based on a standard that called for 3,500 calories per unit per day. This meant a man at moderate muscular work. In fixing the food standard for all families in the Association certain things were taken into account. For instance, frequently the man was not employed, or was in ill health. Many of the families were widows' families. Nevertheless in all families the needs of a man were taken as the unit. The unit standard adopted for A. I. C. P. families was 3,000 calories per unit per day. This gave an allowance that might be called an adequate minimum on which to base the needs of women and children. It was not practical to have a changing unit standard for each family. It was thought safe in the practical working out of the dietaries to use the Atwater scale in spite of the fact that the unit basis was 3,000 calories and not 3,500.

The ration allowance made up from this plan was used with excellent results for eight years before the beginning of the study.

The bills-of-fare possible were fairly satisfactory from the point of view of attractive variety. To administer the food allowance properly meant careful buying, much thought in combining the foods and great care in their preparation. During the time of the study this diet could be purchased at the rate of twenty-seven cents per unit per day. At the present writing, October 1, 1916, the same diet would cost thirty-four cents per unit per day.

The following diet is the basic one for the average family. Calculations for increase according to the size of family are made with these figures as the starting point. It is understood that the prices quoted varied slightly according to locality and season.

RATION ALLOWANCE, 2 ADULTS, 3 CHILDREN—ONE WEEK

Food	*Lbs.*	*Cost*	*Cal.*	*Pro.*	*P_2O_5*	*CaO*	*Fe*	*Acid*	*Base*
Beef Soup Meat	4	$.80	3572	303	6.969	0.2274	0.04545	151.5	
Codfish	1	.12	515	125	3.150	0.1890	0.00504	53.0	
Eggs	1 d.	.35	892	81	2.141	0.5352	0.01695	67.8	
Butterine	1	.25	5115	8	0.204	0.1534			
Milk	14 qts.	1.26	8792	419	26.640	21.0129	0.02989		228.
Cheese	½	.12	997	65	3.230	2.4925		12.9	
Bread	12	.48	14068	506	10.566	1.5497	0.04226	380.0	
Macaroni	1	.08	1624	60	1.624	0.1624	0.00550	43.8	
Rice	1 broken	.06	1591	36	0.907	0.0477	0.00477	43.0	
Oatmeal	3	.10	5049	227	11.683	1.6230	0.04868	162.3	
Sugar	3½	.28	6349						
Beans	2	.20	3128	204	10.197	1.9706	0.06256		156.4
Carrots	4	.12	636	16	1.400	1.0684	0.01018		152.0
Onions	4	.12	796	25	1.910	0.9552	0.00876		24.3
Potatoes	15	.45	4560	122	7.570	0.8664	0.06840		403.2
Apples	4	.12	856	6	0.428	0.1883	0.00428		51.2
Tomatoes	1	.05	103	5	0.0265	0.0896	0.00175		35.0
Prunes	2	.16	2322	16	1.856	0.4644	0.02090		185.8
Cocoa	½	.13	1128	49	2.482	0.3046	0.00564		1.6
Tea	½	.10							
Coffee	½	.12							
Dates	1	.10	1416	9	0.425	0.4243	0.00146		97.0
		5.57	63509	2282	93.4085	34.3250	0.38247	914.3	1334.5

No. of units 3
Cost per unit per month $8.19
" " family per week.... 5.57
" " " " day..... .81
" " unit " " ..... .27

Since the budget calculations are usually made by the month the following table has been arranged on a monthly basis. This table is based upon the ration quoted above. The quantities of food are of course approximate since it would not be practical to weigh each portion. These tables do give, however, the same well-balanced ration as that described in the beginning of this chapter.

Ration Allowances—One Month

1	2	3
1 Adult and 2 Children	1 Adult and 4 Children	2 Adults and 3 Children
1 " " 3 "	2 " " 2 "	1 " " 4 "
2 " " 1 "		
4	**5**	**6**
1 Adult and 6 Children	1 Adult and 7 Children	1 Adult and 8 Children
2 " " 4 "	2 " " 5 "	1 " " 9 "
	2 " " 6 "	2 " " 7 "
		2 " " 8 "

Food	*Amount*	*Amount*	*Amount*	*Amount*	*Amount*	*Amount*
Bread...	34.66 lbs.	39.44 lbs.	52.00 lbs.	62.83 lbs.	73.66 lbs.	98.21 lbs.
Butter ..	6.49 "	6.49 "	6.49 "	8.66 "	8.66 "	10.82 "
Milk....	60.62 qts.	60.62 qts.	60.62 qts.	90.93 qts.	90.93 qts.	90.93 qts.
Eggs....	4.33 doz.	4.33 doz.	4.33 doz.	6.49 doz.	8.66 doz.	8.66 doz.
Cereal ..	12.99 lbs.	17.32 lbs.	21.65 lbs.	25.98 lbs.	28.14 lbs.	28.14 lbs.
Tea, Coffee and Cocoa..	3.24 "	4.33 "	5.41 "	5.41 "	5.41 "	6.49 "
Sugar...	14.07 "	15.15 "	15.15 "	20.56 "	24.89 "	29.22 "
Meat ...	14.07 "	17.32 "	22.19 "	17.32 "	22.73 "	27.06 "
Pot.....	43.3 "	51.96 "	64.95 "	69.28 "	77.94 "	90.93 "
Veg.	51.96 "	51.96 "	47.63 "	64.95 "	82.27 "	95.26 "
Fruit ...	23.81 "	25.98 "	30.31 "	47.63 "	60.62 "	69.28 "

Anyone who has had experience in working with the tenement population knows how intimate a connection exists between food and the more common diseases of poverty. Among our seventy-five families, before the granting of the allowance, record after record reads —"Children anæmic," "Mother suffering from malnutrition." Because of this, special care has been taken with the dietary, and part two will set forth the results.

TABLE FOR CONVERTING UNIT NEEDS INTO DOLLARS AND CENTS

Units	*Cost per month at 0.27 per day*	*Units*	*Cost per month at $.30 per day*
1.0	$ 8.19	1.0	$ 9.10
1.1	9.00	1.1	10.01
1.2	9.83	1.2	10.92
1.3	10.65	1.3	11.63
1.4	11.47	1.4	12.74
1.5	12.29	1.5	13.65
1.6	13.10	1.6	14.56
1.7	13.93	1.7	15.47
1.8	14.74	1.8	16.38
1.9	15.56	1.9	17.29
2.0	16.38	2.0	18.20
2.1	17.20	2.1	19.11
2.2	18.02	2.2	20.02
2.3	18.84	2.3	20.93
2.4	19.66	2.4	21.84
2.5	20.48	2.5	22.75
2.6	21.29	2.6	23.66
2.7	22.11	2.7	24.57

Units	Cost per month at $.27 per day	Units	Cost per month at $.30 per day
2.8	22.93	2.8	$25.48
2.9	23.75	2.9	26.39
3.0	24.57	3.0	27.30
3.1	25.39	3.1	28.21
3.2	26.21	3.2	29.12
3.3	27.02	3.3	30.03
3.4	27.85	3.4	30.94
3.5	28.67	3.5	31.85
3.6	29.48	3.6	32.76
3.7	30.30	3.7	33.67
3.8	31.12	3.8	34.58
3.9	31.94	3.9	35.49
4.0	32.76	4.0	36.40
4.1	33.58	4.1	37.31
4.2	34.40	4.2	38.22
4.3	35.22	4.3	29.13
4.4	36.04	4.4	40.04
4.5	36.86	4.5	40.95
4.6	37.67	4.6	41.86
4.7	38.49	4.7	42.77
4.8	39.31	4.8	43.68
4.9	40.13	4.9	44.59
5.0	40.95	5.0	45.50
5.1	41.77	5.1	46.41
5.2	42.59	5.2	47.32
5.3	43.41	5.3	48.23
5.4	44.23	5.4	49.14
5.5	45.05	5.5	50.05
5.6	45.86	5.6	50.96
5.7	46.68	5.7	51.87
5.8	47.50	5.8	52.78
5.9	48.32	5.9	53.69

Units	Cost per month at $.27 per day	Units	Cost per month at $.30 per day
6.0	49.14	6.0	$54.60
6.1	49.96	6.1	55.51
6.2	50.76	6.2	56.42
6.3	51.60	6.3	57.33
6.4	52.42	6.4	58.24
6.5	53.24	6.5	59.15
6.6	54.05	6.6	60.06
6.7	54.87	6.7	60.97
6.8	55.69	6.8	61.88
6.9	56.51	6.9	62.79
7.0	57.33	7.0	63.70
7.1	58.15	7.1	64.61
7.2	58.97	7.2	65.52
7.3	59.79	7.3	66.43
7.4	60.61	7.4	67.34
7.5	61.45	7.5	68.25
7.6	62.24	7.6	69.16
7.7	63.06	7.7	70.07
7.8	63.88	7.8	70.98
7.9	64.70	7.9	71.69
8.0	65.52	8.0	72.90
8.1	66.34	8.1	73.71
8.2	67.16	8.2	74.62
8.3	67.98	8.3	75.33
8.4	68.60	8.4	76.44
8.5	69.62	8.5	77.35
8.6	70.43	8.6	78.26
8.7	71.25	8.7	79.17
8.8	72.07	8.8	80.08
8.9	72.89	8.9	80.99

Fuel and Light

Information was also sought on this item and an average of all the neighborhoods of the city showed that a tenement apartment of three rooms could be heated and lighted at the rate of $3.25 per month, provided the problem were viewed by the year. According to season it would read something like this:

Winter	$5.00 to $6.00
Spring and Autumn	$2.50 to $3.50
Midsummer	$2.00

In estimating needs for this item this allowance was not increased as the size of the apartments increased, since most of the families made constant use of only three rooms, even though they might possess more.

Clothing

The clothing needs were difficult to decide upon. It is obviously not an easy thing to standardize clothing. During the previous five years, however, there has been in the informal budgets kept by the women much light thrown upon this subject. The tentative sum fixed upon was $2.00 per individual per month. It was understood that this would provide sufficient clothing only on condition that the mother would have time and strength as well as ability to do her own sewing and mending.

It will be understood that the clothing division suggested below is far from satisfying the workers. It is merely an attempt to make the best possible use of a necessarily small clothing allowance. The final figures are based largely on actual practice. The most casual observer will see at once that there is no provision for the small but necessary accessories of dress. The annual clothing allowance for man, woman and four children is as follows: man, $30.20; woman, $28.75; boy 14, $26.05; girl 12, $22.25; girl 6, $17.85; girl 3, $10.75.

The following division of this allowance is quoted from "Clothing the Family," by Mary A. Ditmas. Mrs. Ditmas while sewing teacher of the division did some intensive work in clothing budgets.

DIVISION OF CLOTHING ALLOWANCE FOR MAN, WOMAN AND 4 CHILDREN

MAN

1 suit	$10.00
1 pair trousers	2.00
2 light shirts at $.75 each	1.50
3 colored shirts at $.75 each	2.25
2 pairs shoes	5.00
8 pairs hose at $.15 a pair	1.20

Underwear:	
Winter, 2 suits at $1.00 each	$ 2.00
Summer, 3 suits at $.75 each	2.50
2 hats	1.75
1 necktie	.25
1 pair suspenders	.25
4 collars	.50
2 sets sleeping garments	1.00
Total	$30.20

Clothing for Woman—One Year

Shoes, 2 pairs, $2.50 each	$ 5.00
Repairs	1.25
Aprons, 3 (homemade)	.45
Hats, Winter hat	1.50
Summer hat	1.25
Coats, Winter, 1	3.00
Summer, 1	2.00
Dresses, 2 wash dresses (homemade)	2.00
2 house dresses (homemade)	1.50
Skirts, 1 woolen	2.00
Waists, 2 wash waists (homemade)	1.00
Hosiery, 6 pairs	.60
Gloves, 1 pair cotton	.25
1 pair woolen	.75
Underwear:	
Winter, three union suits, $.75 each	2.25
Summer, three union suits, $.25 each	.75
2 corset covers (homemade)	.75
2 flannelette skirts (homemade)	.50
2 night dresses (homemade)	.70
1 pair corsets	1.00
Linen	.50
Total	$28.75

Girl of Twelve Years

Shoes, 2 pair at $2.00	$ 4.00
Repairs	1.25
1 pair rubbers	.65
Gloves, 2 pair woolen at $.25	.50
Hats, Winter (trimmed at home)	1.00
Summer (trimmed at home)	.75
Coats, Winter	2.50
Summer	1.00
Sweater (homemade)	1.25
Dresses, one woolen dress	1.50
3 wash dresses (homemade) (at $.50)	1.50
Skirts, 1 woolen skirt (homemade)	1.00
Waists, 2 middy blouses (homemade)	.75
Hosiery, 6 pair at $.10	.60
Underwear:	
Winter, 3 union suits at $.50	1.50
Summer, 3 union suits at $.10	.30
2 flannelette skirts (homemade)	.80
2 night dresses (homemade)	.60
2 white muslin petticoats (homemade)	.30
Ribbons, etc	.50
Total	$22.25

Boy of Fourteen Years

Overcoats, winter, one coat	$ 4.50
One sweater	1.00
Hats, two	.75
Suits, one	2.50
Trousers, 3 wash trousers	1.50
One woolen trouser	.75
Blouses, 4 cotton (homemade) at $.20	.80
3 outing blouses	1.50
Gloves, 1 pair	.25
Hosiery, 12 pairs stockings	1.20

Shoes, 3 pairs at $1.75	$ 5.25
Repairs	2.00
Rubbers	.60
Underwear:	
Summer, 3 suits at $.25	.75
Winter, 3 suits at $.75	2.25
Underbodies (homemade)	.45
Total	$26.05

Girl of Six Years

Shoes, 2 pairs at $1.25	$ 2.50
Repairs	1.25
Rubbers	.60
Gloves, 2 pairs woolen at $.25	.50
Hats, 1 felt (trimmed at home)	.75
1 summer (trimmed at home)	.50
Coats, winter (made at home)	1.75
Summer (made at home)	1.00
Sweater (made at home)	.50
Dresses, 2 woolen (homemade)	1.50
4 wash dresses (homemade)	1.75
Hosiery, 6 pairs at $.10	.60
Underwear, 3 underwaists (homemade)	.35
Winter, 3 union suits at $.50	1.50
Summer, 3 shirts	.30
4 pairs muslin drawers (homemade)	.60
2 flannelette skirts (homemade)	.50
2 cotton petticoats	.50
2 nightgowns	.40
Ribbons	.50
Total	$17.85

Girl of Three Years

Shoes, 2 pairs at $1.25	$ 2.50
Repairs	.75
Hats, 2 caps at $.25	.50

Suits or dresses:	
4 wash suits or dresses (homemade)	$ 1.50
4 pairs rompers (homemade)	.60
Coats, 1 winter	2.00
1 summer (homemade)	1.00
Hosiery, 4 pairs stockings	.40
Underwear, 3 winter union suits at $.25	.75
3 summer union suits at $.15	.45
2 nightgowns (homemade)	.30
Total	$10.75

SUNDRIES

The workers realized that the provision possible for this item would be inadequate. The amount finally fixed was $1.00 each for the first three members of the family per month, and fifty cents each for each additional person. This provided only for the barest necessities. This item had also to include provision for insurance. The Association advocates insurance only for the breadwinner. Most of the families, however, make payments for children's insurance.

PART II

THE SEVENTY-FIVE EXPENSE ACCOUNTS IN DETAIL

The figures on the following pages give the main items in the budget, and the actual expenditures for these items in each family. The estimate spoken of has been slightly modified to meet individual needs. The estimate for sundries at the time the study was made was $2.00 per family per month. The increase according to size of family came later. The sum paid for insurance by each family has been added to the estimate for sundries. When the $2.00 rate was in use it was understood that special needs must be provided for through some other source.

YEARLY SUMMARY OF SEVENTY-FIVE BUDGETS

Family No. 1, Woman, 2 children, 13, 8

	Est. of needs 1 mo.	*Est. of needs 12 mo.*	*Act. Exp. 12 mo.*	*Act. Inc. 12 mo.*	*Act. over budget*	*Act. under budget*	*Summary*
Rent	free	free	free	$386.00			
Food	17.33	207.96	289.48		$81.52		
F. & L.	3.25	39.00	24.24			$14.76	Bal. end
Clo.	6.00	72.00	29.82			42.18	of 12 mo.
Sund.	3.30	39.60	40.90		1.30		$1.56
	$29.88	$358.56	$384.44	$386.00	$82.82	$56.94	

Family No. 2, Woman, 2 children, 11, 5

	Est. of needs 1 mo.	*Est. of needs 12 mo.*	*Act. Exp. 12 mo.*	*Act. Inc. 12 mo.*	*Act. over budget*	*Act. under budget*	*Summary*
Rent	$13.00	$156.00	$156.00	$520.33			
Food	17.33	207.96	240.89		$32.93		
F. & L.	3.25	39.00	17.15			$21.85	
Clo.	6.00	72.00	33.83			38.17	Bal. end
Sund.	3.07	36.84	61.29		24.45		of 12 mo.
Baby's Bd.			2.30		2.30		$8.87
	$42.65	$511.80	$511.46	$520.33	$59.68	$60.02	

Family No. 3, Woman, 2 children, 15, 11

	Est. of needs 1 mo.	*Est. of needs 12 mo.*	*Act. Exp. 12 mo.*	*Act. Inc. 12 mo.*	*Act. over budget*	*Act. under budget*	*Summary*
Rent	free	free	free	$269.96			
Food	$17.33	$209.96	$193.18			$16.78	
F. & L.	3.25	39.00	43.21		$ 4.21		Bal. end
Clo.	6.00	72.00	15.89			56.11	of 12 mo.
Sund.	3.00	36.00	15.16			20.84	$2.52
	$29.58	$356.96	$267.44	$269.96	$ 4.21	$93.73	

Family No. 4, Woman, 3 children, 10, 9, 6

	Est. of needs 1 mo.	*Est. of needs 12 mo.*	*Act. Exp. 12 mo.*	*Act. Inc. 12 mo.*	*Act. over budget*	*Act. under budget*	*Summary*
Rent	$13.00	$156.00	$156.05	$569.11	$ .05		
Food	18.02	216.24	286.70		70.46		
F. & L.	3.25	39.00	41.36		2.36		Bal. end
Clo.	8.00	96.00	39.97			$56.03	of 12 mo.
Sund.	5.00	39.60	42.19		2.59		$2.84
	$47.27	$546.84	$566.27	$569.11	$75.46	$56.03	

Family No. 5, Woman, 3 children, 9, 6, 4

	Est. of needs 1 mo.	*Est. of needs 12 mo.*	*Act. Exp. 12 mo.*	*Act. Inc. 12 mo.*	*Act. over budget*	*Act. under budget*	*Summary*
Rent	$12.00	$144.00	$150.00	$483.68	$ 6.00		
Food	17.33	207.96	187.36			$20.60	
F. & L.	3.25	39.00	29.19			9.81	Bal. end
Clo.	6.00	72.00	60.39			11.61	of 12 mo.
Sund.	3.73	44.76	49.16		4.40		$7.58
	$42.31	$507.72	$476.10	$483.68	$10.40	$42.02	

	Est. of needs 1 mo.	*Est. of needs 12 mo.*	*Act. Exp. 12 mo.*	*Act. Inc. 12 mo.*	*Act. over budget*	*Act. under budget*	*Summary*
Family No. 6, Woman, 3 children, 8, 6, 4							
Rent	$10.00	$120.00	$120.00	$515.61			
Food	18.07	216.84	256.05		$39.21		
F. & L.	3.25	39.00	27.19			$11.81	Bal. end
Clo	8.00	96.00	47.37			48.63	of 12 mo.
Sund	4.39	52.68	64.95		12.27		$.05
	$43.71	$524.52	$515.56	$515.61	$51.48	$60.44	
Family No. 7, Woman, 3 children, 8, 6, 4							
Rent	$10.00	$120.00	$122.00	$602.44	$ 2.00		
Food	17.20	206.40	219.72		13.32		
F. & L.	3.25	39.00	31.77			$ 7.23	Bal. end
Clo	8.00	96.00	47.06			48.94	of 12 mo.
Sund	5.25	63.00	134.49		71.49		$47.40
	$43.70	$524.40	$555.04	$602.44	$86.81	$56.17	
Family No. 8, Woman, 3 children, 17, 11, 5							
Rent	$11.00	$132.00	$151.00	$701.36	$19.00		
Food	27.85	334.20	307.68			$26.52	
F. & L.	3.25	39.00	16.85			22.15	Bal. end
Clo	10.00	120.00	79.53			40.47	of 12 mo.
Sund	7.68	92.16	126.65		34.49		$19.65
	$59.78	$717.36	$681.71	$701.36	$53.49	$89.14	
Family No. 9, Woman, 3 children, 14, 10, 8							
Rent	$12.00	$144.00	$135.00	$535.03		$ 9.00	
Food	20.27	243.24	220.76			22.46	
F. & L.	3.25	39.00	32.59			6.41	Bal. end
Clo	8.00	96.00	43.54			52.46	of 12 mo.
Sund	3.47	41.64	79.90		$38.26		$23.22
	$46.99	$563.88	$511.81	$535.03	$38.26	$90.33	
Family No. 10, Woman, 3 children, 11, 8, 6							
Rent	$16.00	$192.00	$184.00	$594.46		$ 8.00	
Food	18.84	226.08	291.49		$65.41		
F. & L.	3.25	39.00	28.31			10.69	Bal. end
Clo	8.00	96.00	35.18			60.82	of 12 mo.
Sund	3.38	40.56	47.27		6.71		$8.21
	$49.47	$593.64	$586.25	$594.46	$72.12	$79.51	

Family No. 11, Woman, 3 children, 11, 10, 5

	Est. of needs 1 mo.	Est. of needs 12 mo.	Act. Exp. 12 mo.	Act. Inc. 12 mo.	Act. over budget	Act. under budget	Summary
Rent	$ 8.00	$ 96.00	$ 84.00	$491.05		$12.00	
Food	21.84	262.08	259.35			2.72	
F. & L.	3.25	39.00	33.61			5.39	Bal. end
Clo.	8.00	96.00	57.13			38.87	of 12 mo.
Sund.	2.91	34.92	56.28		$21.36		$.68
	$44.00	$528.00	$490.37	$491.05	$21.36	$58.98	

Family No. 12, Woman, 3 children, 8, 6, 4

	Est. of needs 1 mo.	Est. of needs 12 mo.	Act. Exp. 12 mo.	Act. Inc. 12 mo.	Act. over budget	Act. under budget	Summary
Rent	$13.00	$156.00	$156.00	$572.27			
Food	20.02	240.24	261.47		$21.23		
F. & L.	3.25	39.00	30.40			$ 8.60	Bal. end
Clo.	8.00	96.00	72.91			23.09	of 12 mo.
Sund.	3.60	43.20	51.24		8.04		$.25
	$47.87	$572.02	$572.02	$572.27	$29.27	$31.69	

Family No. 13, Woman, 3 children, 12, 10, 7

	Est. of needs 1 mo.	Est. of needs 12 mo.	Act. Exp. 12 mo.	Act. Inc. 12 mo.	Act. over budget	Act. under budget	Summary
Rent	$21.00	$252.00	$252.00	$731.48			
Food	20.48	245.76	336.11		$90.35		
F. & L.	3.25	39.00	35.83			$ 3.27	Bal. end
Clo.	8.00	96.00	48.00			48.00	of 12 mo.
Sund.	3.95	47.40	56.21		8.81		$3.33
	$56.68	$680.16	$728.15	$731.48	$99.16	$51.27	

Family No. 14, Woman, 3 children, 12, 10, 7

	Est. of needs 1 mo.	Est. of needs 12 mo.	Act. Exp. 12 mo.	Act. Inc. 12 mo.	Act. over budget	Act. under budget	Summary
Rent	$18.00	$216.00	$216.00	$711.14			
Food	20.48	245.76	313.76		$68.00		
F. & L.	3.25	39.00	36.85			$ 2.15	
Clo.	8.00	96.00	63.45			32.55	Bal. end
Sund.	2.00	24.00	38.50		14.50		of 12 mo.
C. F.	3.90	46.80	35.80			11.00	$6.78
	$55.63	$667.56	$704.36	$711.14	$82.50	$45.70	

Family No. 15, Woman, 3 children, 10, 9, 3

	Est. of needs 1 mo.	Est. of needs 12 mo.	Act. Exp. 12 mo.	Act. Inc. 12 mo.	Act. over budget	Act. under budget	Summary
Rent	$11.00	$132.00	$132.00	$516.16			
Food	22.11	265.32	259.24			$ 6.08	
F. & L.	3.25	39.00	32.81			6.19	Bal. end
Clo.	8.00	96.00	53.44			42.56	of 12 mo.
Sund.	2.00	24.00	32.66		$ 8.66		$6.01
	$46.36	$556.32	$510.15	$516.16	$ 8.66	$54.83	

Family No. 16, Woman, 3 children, 12, 8, 6

	Est. of needs 1 mo.	*12 mo.*	*Act. Exp. 12 mo.*	*Act. Inc. 12 mo.*	*Act. over budget*	*Act. under budget*	*Summary*
Rent	$13.00	$156.00	$143.00	$642.86		$13.00	
Food	28.21	338.52	306.51			32.01	
F. & L.	3.25	39.00	32.55			6.45	
Clo.	8.00	96.00	56.53			39.47	Bal. end
Sund.	3.66	43.92	63.72		$19.80		of 12 mo.
C. F.	4.60	55.20	31.25			23.95	$9.30
	$60.72	$728.64	$633.56	$642.86	$19.80	$114.85	

Family No. 17, Woman, 3 children, 10, 8, 5

	Est. of needs 1 mo.	*12 mo.*	*Act. Exp. 12 mo.*	*Act. Inc. 12 mo.*	*Act. over budget*	*Act. under budget*	*Summary*
Rent	$14.00	$168.00	$ 84.00	$503.29		$84.00	
Food	18.02	216.24	270.10		$53.86		
F. & L.	3.25	39.00	36.23			2.77	Bal. end
Clo.	8.00	96.00	57.97			38.03	of 12 mo.
Sund.	3.50	42.00	44.53		2.53		$10.46
	$46.77	$561.24	$492.83	$503.29	$56.39	$124.80	

Family No. 18, Woman, 3 children, 14, 11, 4

	Est. of needs 1 mo.	*12 mo.*	*Act. Exp. 12 mo.*	*Act. Inc. 12 mo.*	*Act. over budget*	*Act. under budget*	*Summary*
Rent	$10.00	$120.00	$ 99.25	$466.25		$20.75	
Food	19.66	235.92	230.62			5.30	
F. & L.	3.25	39.00	39.77		$ .77		Bal. end
Clo.	8.00	96.00	54.74			41.26	of 12 mo.
Sund.	2.00	24.00	30.42		6.42		$11.45
	$42.91	$514.92	$454.80	$466.25	$ 7.19	$67.31	

Family No. 19, Woman, 3 children, 12, 10, 9

	Est. of needs 1 mo.	*12 mo.*	*Act. Exp. 12 mo.*	*Act. Inc. 12 mo.*	*Act. over budget*	*Act. under budget*	*Summary*
Rent	$13.00	$156.00	$149.50	$526.65		$ 6.50	
Food	18.44	221.28	241.29		$20.01		
F. & L.	3.25	39.00	24.81			14.19	Bal. end
Clo.	8.00	96.00	57.35			38.65	of 12 mo.
Sund.	2.65	31.80	42.51		10.71		$11.19
	$45.34	$544.08	$515.46	$526.65	$30.72	$59.34	

Family No. 20, Woman 3 children, 11, 9, 6,

	Est. of needs 1 mo.	*12 mo.*	*Act. Exp. 12 mo.*	*Act. Inc. 12 mo.*	*Act. over budget*	*Act. under budget*	*Summary*
Rent	$ 1.00	$ 12.00	$ 12.00	$494.61			
Food	18.02	216.24	290.00		$73.76		
F. & L.	3.25	39.00	36.90			$ 2.10	Bal. end
Clo.	8.00	96.00	65.05			30.95	of 12 mo.
Sund.	3.73	44.76	75.25		30.49		$15.41
	$34.00	$408.00	$479.20	$494.61	$104.25	$33.05	

	Est. of needs 1 mo.	*12 mo.*	*Act. Exp. 12 mo.*	*Act. Inc. 12 mo.*	*Act. over budget*	*Act. under budget*	*Summary*
Family No. 21, Woman, 3 children, 14, 11, 8							
Rent	$ 8.00	$ 96.00	$111.00	$554.63	$15.00		
Food	19.65	235.92	277.02		41.10		
F. & L.	3.25	39.00	29.69			$ 9.31	Bal. end
Clo.	8.00	96.00	48.58			47.42	of 12 mo.
Sund.	3.95	47.40	69.56		22.16		$18.78
	$42.85	$514.32	$535.85	$554.63	$78.26	$56.73	

	Est. of needs 1 mo.	*12 mo.*	*Act. Exp. 12 mo.*	*Act. Inc. 12 mo.*	*Act. over budget*	*Act. under budget*	*Summary*
Family No. 22, Woman, 3 children, 10, 7, 4							
Rent	$10.00	$120.00	$105.00	$415.89		$15.00	
Food	25.39	304.68	237.18			67.50	
F. & L.	3.25	39.00	43.06		$ 4.06		Bal. end
Clo.	10.00	120.00	11.76			108.24	of 12 mo.
Sund.	4.00	48.00	17.32			30.68	$1.57
	$52.64	$631.68	$414.32	$415.89	$ 4.06	$221.42	

	Est. of needs 1 mo.	*12 mo.*	*Act. Exp. 12 mo.*	*Act. Inc. 12 mo.*	*Act. over budget*	*Act. under budget*	*Summary*
Family No. 23, Woman, 3 children, 11, 8, 5							
Rent	$15.00	$180.00	$180.00	$698.86			
Food	24.57	294.84	311.14		$16.30		
F. & L.	3.25	39.00	41.59		2.59		
Clo.	8.00	96.00	42.29			$53.71	Bal. end
Sund.	4.50	54.00	98.77		44.77		of 12 mo.
C. F.	2.60	31.20	22.00			9.20	$3.07
	$57.92	$695.04	$695.79	$698.86	$63.66	$62.91	

	Est. of needs 1 mo.	*12 mo.*	*Act. Exp. 12 mo.*	*Act. Inc. 12 mo.*	*Act. over budget*	*Act. under budget*	*Summary*
Family No. 24, Woman, 3 children, 12, 11, 10							
Rent	$13.00	$156.00	$149.50	$559.09		$ 6.50	
Food	20.47	245.64	267.18		$21.54		
F. & L.	3.25	39.00	25.06			13.94	Bal. end
Clo.	8.00	96.00	78.20			17.80	of 12 mo.
Sund.	3.50	42.00	32.66			9.34	$6.49
	$48.22	$578.64	$552.60	$559.09	$21.54	$47.58	

	Est. of needs 1 mo.	*12 mo.*	*Act. Exp. 12 mo.*	*Act. Inc. 12 mo.*	*Act. over budget*	*Act. under budget*	*Summary*
Family No. 25, Woman, 3 children, 14, 10, 8							
Rent	$11.00	$132.00	$138.00	$657.66	$ 6.00		
Food	29.48	353.76	322.37			$31.39	
F. & L.	3.25	39.00	34.35			4.65	Bal. end
Clo.	10.00	120.00	60.42			59.58	of 12 mo.
Sund.	4.60	55.20	92.21		37.01		$10.31
	$58.33	$699.96	$647.35	$657.66	$41.01	$95.62	

	Est. of needs 1 mo.	*12 mo.*	*Act. Exp. 12 mo.*	*Act. Inc. 12 mo.*	*Act. over budget*	*Act. under budget*	*Summary*
Family No. 26, Woman, 3 children, 10, 8, 5							
Rent	$14.00	$168.00	$157.00	$651.46		$11.00	
Food	24.47	293.64	309.12		$15.48		
F. & L.	3.25	39.00	17.83			21.17	Bal. end
Clo.	8.00	96.00	71.83			24.17	of 12 mo.
Sund.	3.51	42.12	91.64		49.52		$4.04
	$53.23	$638.76	$647.42	$651.46	$65.00	$56.34	
Family No. 27, Woman, 3 children, 15, 10, 9							
Rent	$14.00	$168.00	$179.50	$608.88	$11.50		
Food	22.11	265.32	238.63			$26.69	
F. & L.	3.25	39.00	36.18			2.82	Bal. end
Clo.	8.00	96.00	101.71		5.71		of 12 mo.
Sund.	3.00	36.00	51.32		15.32		$1.54
	$50.36	$704.32	$607.34	$608.88	$32.53	$29.51	
Family No. 28, Woman, 3 children, 12, 10, 7							
Rent	$13.00	$156.00	$156.00	$592.74			
Food	22.11	265.32	259.55			$ 5.77	
F. & L.	3.25	39.00	26.88			12.12	Bal. end
Clo.	8.00	96.00	43.69			52.31	of 12 mo.
Sund.	2.00	24.00	65.04		$41.04		$35.58
	$48.36	$580.32	$551.16	$592.74	$41.04	$71.20	
Family No. 29, Woman, 3 children, 11, 8, 6							
Rent	$10.00	$120.00	$115.00	$396.55		$ 5.00	
Food	19.66	235.92	193.67			42.25	
F. & L.	3.25	39.00	15.95			23.05	Bal. end
Clo.	8.00	96.00	34.81			61.19	of 12 mo.
Sund.	3.30	39.60	33.41			6.19	$3.71
	$44.21	$530.52	$392.84	$396.55		$137.68	
Family No. 30, Woman, 4 children, 15, 13, 12, 10							
Rent	$19.00	$228.00	$208.25	$671.38		$19.75	
Food	27.84	334.08	342.63		$ 8.55		
F. & L.	3.25	39.00	39.44		.44		Bal. end
Clo.	10.00	120.00	31.31			88.69	of 12 mo.
Sund.	2.00	24.00	47.15		23.15		$2.60
	$52.09	$745.08	$668.78	$671.38	$32.14	$108.44	

Family No. 31, Woman, 4 children, 13, 11, 9, 7

	Est. of needs 1 mo.	*Est. of needs 12 mo.*	*Act. Exp. 12 mo.*	*Act. Inc. 12 mo.*	*Act. over budget*	*Act. under budget*	*Summary*
Rent	$14.00	$168.00	$148.00	$515.10	$26.38	$20.00	
Food	24.57	294.84	220.55			74.29	
F. & L.	3.25	39.00	18.92			20.08	Bal. end
Clo.	10.00	120.00	55.59			64.41	of 12 mo.
Sund.	3.73	44.76	71.14				$.90
	$55.55	$666.60	$514.20	$515.10	$26.38	$178.78	

Family No. 32, Woman, 4 children, 10, 8, 6, 5

	Est. of needs 1 mo.	*Est. of needs 12 mo.*	*Act. Exp. 12 mo.*	*Act. Inc. 12 mo.*	*Act. over budget*	*Act. under budget*	*Summary*
Rent	$12.00	$144.00	$132.00	$502.07		$12.00	
Food	22.93	255.16	265.07		$ 9.91		
F. & L.	3.25	39.00	22.65			16.35	Bal. end
Clo.	10.00	120.00	47.19			72.81	of 12 mo.
Sund.	4.00	48.00	35.15			12.85	$.01
	$52.18	$606.16	$502.06	$502.07	$ 9.91	$114.01	

Family No. 33, Woman, 4 children, 12, 9, 8, 6

	Est. of needs 1 mo.	*Est. of needs 12 mo.*	*Act. Exp. 12 mo.*	*Act. Inc. 12 mo.*	*Act. over budget*	*Act. under budget*	*Summary*
Rent	$21.00	$252.00	$243.00	$624.60		$ 9.00	
Food	22.11	265.32	245.70			19.62	
F. & L.	3.25	39.00	20.83			14.17	Bal. end
Clo.	10.00	120.00	28.01			91.99	of 12 mo.
Sund.	6.98	83.76	78.19			5.57	$4.87
	$63.34	$760.08	$619.73	$624.60		$140.35	

Family No. 34, Woman, 4 children, 15, 13, 11, 4

	Est. of needs 1 mo.	*Est. of needs 12 mo.*	*Act. Exp. 12 mo.*	*Act. Inc. 12 mo.*	*Act. over budget*	*Act. under budget*	*Summary*
Rent	$12.00	$144.00	$176.00	$752.66	$32.00		
Food	34.40	412.80	385.54			$27.26	
F. & L.	3.25	39.00	39.02		.02		Bal. end
Clo.	10.00	120.00	70.36			49.64	of 12 mo.
Sund.	4.00	48.00	79.32		31.32		$2.42
	$63.65	$763.80	$750.24	$752.66	$63.34	$76.90	

Family No. 35, Woman, 4 children, 9, 7, 6, 4

	Est. of needs 1 mo.	*Est. of needs 12 mo.*	*Act. Exp. 12 mo.*	*Act. Inc. 12 mo.*	*Act. over budget*	*Act. under budget*	*Summary*
Rent	$14.00	$168.00	$168.00	$625.39			
Food	20.47	245.64	251.08		$ 5.44		
F. & L.	3.25	39.00	29.65			$ 9.35	Bal. end
Clo.	9.00	108.00	88.57			19.43	of 12 mo.
Sund.	3.95	47.40	81.06		33.66		$7.03
	$50.67	$608.04	$618.36	$625.39	$39.10	$28.78	

Family No. 36, Woman, 4 children, 16, 11, 9, 8

	Est. of needs 1 mo.	12 mo.	Act. Exp. 12 mo.	Act. Inc. 12 mo.	Act. over budget	Act. under budget	Summary
Rent	$13.50	$162.00	$161.65	$647.47		$ .35	
Food	27.02	324.24	324.87		$ .63		
F. & L.	3.25	39.00	54.50		15.40		Bal. end
Clo.	10.00	120.00	52.37			67.63	of 12 mo.
Sund.	2.00	24.00	33.51		9.51		$20.67
	$55.77	$669.24	$626.80	$647.47	$25.54	$67.98	

Family No. 37, Woman, 4 children, 14, 13, 11, 9

	Est. of needs 1 mo.	12 mo.	Act. Exp. 12 mo.	Act. Inc. 12 mo.	Act. over budget	Act. under budget	Summary
Rent			$ 18.00	$406.26	$18.00		
Food	$22.11	$265.32	258.24			$ 7.08	
F. & L.	3.25	39.00	34.70			4.30	Bal. end
Clo.	10.00	120.00	55.36			64.64	of 12 mo.
Sund.	3.30	39.60	39.45			.15	$.51
	$38.66	$463.92	$405.75	$406.26	$18.00	$76.17	

Family No. 38, Woman, 4 children, 17, 15, 13, 11

	Est. of needs 1 mo.	12 mo.	Act. Exp. 12 mo.	Act. Inc. 12 mo.	Act. over budget	Act. under budget	Summary
Rent	$10.00	$120.00	$125.00	$566.54	$ 5.00		
Food	22.93	275.16	280.76		5.60		
F. & L.	3.25	39.00	25.50			$13.50	Bal. end
Clo.	8.00	96.00	47.98			48.02	of 12 mo.
Sund.	3.50	42.00	87.24		45.24		$.06
	$47.68	$572.16	$566.48	$566.54	$55.84	$61.52	

Family No. 39, Woman, 4 children, 7, 6, 5, 3

	Est. of needs 1 mo.	12 mo.	Act. Exp. 12 mo.	Act. Inc. 12 mo.	Act. over budget	Act. under budget	Summary
Rent	$13.00	$156.00	$156.00	$615.82			
Food	21.35	256.20	314.76		$58.56		
F. & L.	3.25	39.00	30.31			$ 8.69	Bal. end
Clo.	10.00	120.00	63.29			56.71	of 12 mo.
Sund.	3.40	40.80	48.99		8.19		$2.47
	$51.00	$612.00	$613.35	$615.82	$66.75	$65.40	

Family No. 40, Woman, 4 children, 13, 11, 8, 4

	Est. of needs 1 mo.	12 mo.	Act. Exp. 12 mo.	Act. Inc. 12 mo.	Act. over budget	Act. under budget	Summary
Rent	$13.00	$156.00	$156.00	$573.39			
Food	25.75	309.00	319.16		$10.16		
F. & L.	3.25	39.00	16.81			$22.19	Bal. end
Clo.	4.00	48.00	40.38			7.62	of 12 mo
Sund.	3.00	36.00	70.43		34.43		$29.38
	$49.00	$588.00	$602.78	$573.39	$44.59	$29.81	

	Est. of needs 1 mo.	*Est. of needs 12 mo.*	*Act. Exp. 12 mo.*	*Act. Inc. 12 mo.*	*Act. over budget*	*Act. under budget*	*Summary*
Family No. 41, Woman, 4 children, 9, 7, 5, 3							
Rent	$12.00	$144.00	$144.00	$542.10			
Food	19.13	229.56	206.19			$23.36	
F. & L.	3.25	39.00	35.12			3.88	
Clo.	10.00	120.00	49.41			70.59	Bal. end
Sund.	3.95	47.40	73.46		$26.06		of 12 mo.
Nur. fees	1.30	15.60	32.45		16.85		$1.47
	$49.63	$595.56	$540.63	$542.10	$42.91	$97.83	
Family No. 42, Woman, 4 children, 16, 13, 9, 5							
Rent	$12.00	$144.00	$136.00	$685.78		$ 8.00	
Food	29.48	353.76	349.96			3.80	
F. & L.	3.25	39.00	45.54		$ 6.54		
Clo.	10.00	120.00	65.49			54.51	Bal. end
Sund.	3.73	44.36	56.85		12.09		of 12 mo.
C. F.	2.40	28.80	29.68		.88		$2.26
	$60.86	$730.32	$683.52	$685.78	$19.51	$66.31	
Family No. 43, Woman, 4 children, 14, 12, 9, 5							
Rent	$ 7.50	$ 90.00	$125.00	$639.05	$35.00		
Food	30.03	360.36	339.10			$21.26	
F. & L.	3.25	39.00	20.18			18.82	Bal. end
Clo.	10.00	120.00	80.58			39.42	of 12 mo.
Sund.	2.00	24.00	63.90		38.90		$10.29
	$52.78	$633.36	$628.76	$639.05	$74.90	$79.50	
Family No. 44, Woman, 4 children, 12, 8, 5, 3							
Rent	$11.00	$132.00	$126.50	$544.06		$ 5.50	
Food	22.11	265.32	270.73		$ 5.41		
F. & L.	3.25	39.00	22.49			16.51	Bal. end
Clo.	10.00	120.00	54.61			65.39	of 12 mo.
Sund.	3.52	42.24	67.02		24.78		$2.71
	$49.88	$598.56	$541.35	$544.06	$30.19	$87.40	
Family No. 45, Woman, 4 children, 12, 9, 5, 2							
Rent	$ 5.00	$ 60.00	$ 80.00	$557.55	$20.00		
Food	22.11	265.32	291.37		26.05		
F. & L.	3.25	39.00	19.89			$19.11	Bal. end
Clo.	10.00	120.00	75.72			44.28	of 12 mo.
Sund.	4.38	52.56	82.79		30.23		$7.78
	$44.74	$549.78	$549.78	$557.55	$76.28	$63.39	

Family No. 46, Woman, 4 children, 16, 10, 8, 6

	Est. of needs 1 mo.	*12 mo.*	*Act. Exp. 12 mo.*	*Act. Inc. 12 mo.*	*Act. over budget*	*Act. under budget*	*Summary*
Rent	$13.00	$156.00	$147.00	$751.50		$ 9.00	
Food	27.84	334.08	332.67			1.41	
F. & L.	3.25	39.00	31.26			7.74	
Clo.	10.00	120.00	87.76			32.24	Bal. end
Sund.	2.00	24.00	77.47		$53.47		of 12 mo.
C. F.	2.60	31.20	53.20		22.00		$22.14
	$58.69	$704.28	$729.36	$751.50	$75.47	$50.39	

Family No. 47, Woman, 4 children, 15, 13, 11, 6

	Est. of needs 1 mo.	*12 mo.*	*Act. Exp. 12 mo.*	*Act. Inc. 12 mo.*	*Act. over budget*	*Act. under budget*	*Summary*
Rent	$14.00	$168.00	$168.00	$505.38			
Food	26.21	314.52	262.76			$51.76	
F. & L.	3.25	39.00	5.95			33.05	Bal. end
Clo.	10.00	120.00	26.05			93.95	of 12 mo.
Sund.	2.00	24.00	25.20		$ 1.20		$17.42
	$55.46	$665.52	$487.96	$505.38	$ 1.20	$178.76	

Family No. 48, Woman, 4 children, 12, 9, 7, 5

	Est. of needs 1 mo.	*12 mo.*	*Act. Exp. 12 mo.*	*Act. Inc. 12 mo.*	*Act. over budget*	*Act. under budget*	*Summary*
Rent	$11.00	$132.00	$122.00	$550.32		$10.00	
Food	22.95	275.40	282.49		$ 7.09		
F. & L.	3.25	39.00	38.64			.36	Bal. end
Clo.	10.00	120.00	60.76			59.24	of 12 mo.
Sund.	2.00	24.00	45.55		21.55		$.88
	$49.20	$590.40	$549.44	$550.32	$28.64	$69.60	

Family No. 49, Woman, 5 children, 15, 13, 9, 7, 5

	Est. of needs 1 mo.	*12 mo.*	*Act. Exp. 12 mo.*	*Act. Inc. 12 mo.*	*Act. over budget*	*Act. under budget*	*Summary*
Rent	$15.00	$180.00	$168.75	$716.51		$11.25	
Food	32.30	387.60	334.56			53.04	
F. & L.	3.25	39.00	43.46		$ 4.46		Bal. end
Clo.	12.00	144.00	73.63			70.37	of 12 mo.
Sund.	4.60	55.20	96.69		41.49		$.58
	$67.15	$805.80	$717.09	$716.51	$45.95	$134.66	

Family No. 50, Woman, 5 children, 18, 12, 9, 7, 4

	Est. of needs 1 mo.	*12 mo.*	*Act. Exp. 12 mo.*	*Act. Inc. 12 mo.*	*Act. over budget*	*Act. under budget*	*Summary*
Rent	$13.00	$156.00	$195.00	$634.80	$39.00		
Food	27.02	324.24	298.49			$25.75	
F. & L.	3.25	39.00	31.89			7.11	Bal. end
Clo.	6.00	72.00	99.28		27.28		of 12 mo.
Sund.	2.88	34.56	46.09		11.53		$35.95
	$52.15	$625.80	$670.75	$634.80	$77.81	$32.86	

Family No. 51, Woman, 5 children, 15, 14, 11, 6, 5

	Est. of needs 1 mo.	*12 mo.*	*Act. Exp. 12 mo.*	*Act. Inc. 12 mo.*	*Act. over budget*	*Act. under budget*	*Summary*
Rent	$10.50	$126.00	$136.00	$691.03	$10.00		
Food	31.12	373.44	376.01		2.57		
F. & L.	3.25	39.00	35.35			$3.65	Bal. end
Clo.	12.00	144.00	91.33			52.67	of 12 mo.
Sund.	2.00	24.00	52.03		28.03		$.31
	$58.87	$706.44	$690.72	$691.03	$40.60	$56.32	

Family No. 52, Woman, 5 children, 19, 11, 10, 8, 5

	Est. of needs 1 mo.	*12 mo.*	*Act. Exp. 12 mo.*	*Act. Inc. 12 mo.*	*Act. over budget*	*Act. under budget*	*Summary*
Rent	$15.00	$165.00	$150.00	$832.16		$15.00	
Food	26.50	291.50	285.94			5.56	
F. & L.	3.25	35.75	35.05			.70	Bal. end
Clo.	12.00	132.00	137.73		$ 5.73		of 12 mo.
Sund.	6.00	66.00	143.49		77.49		$79.95
	$62.75	$690.25	$752.21	$832.16	$83.22	$21.26	

Family No. 53, Woman, 5 children, 11, 9, 7, 5, 4

	Est. of needs 1 mo.	*12 mo.*	*Act. Exp. 12 mo.*	*Act. Inc. 12 mo.*	*Act. over budget*	*Act. under budget*	*Summary*
Rent	$ 9.50	$114.00	$ 96.50	$482.50		$17.50	
Food	22.11	265.33	278.27		$12.94		
F. & L.	3.25	39.00	22.27			16.73	Bal. end
Clo.	10.00	120.00	70.03			49.97	of 12 mo.
Sund.	2.00	24.00	17.11			6.89	$1.68
	$46.86	$562.33	$484.18	$482.50	$12.94	$91.09	

Family No. 54, Woman, 5 children, 7, 6, 5, 4, 2

	Est. of needs 1 mo.	*12 mo.*	*Act. Exp. 12 mo.*	*Act. Inc. 12 mo.*	*Act. over budget*	*Act. under budget*	*Summary*
Rent	$10.00	$120.00	$120.00	$485.41			
Food	23.00	276.00	278.08		$ 2.08		
F. & L.	3.25	39.00	18.10			$20.90	Bal. end
Clo.	10.00	120.00	39.60			80.40	of 12 mo.
Sund.	3.00	36.00	23.73			12.27	$5.90
	$49.25	$591.00	$479.51	$485.41	$ 2.08	$113.57	

Family No. 55, Woman, 5 children, 13, 11, 7, 4, 20 months

	Est. of needs 1 mo.	*12 mo.*	*Act. Exp. 12 mo.*	*Act. Inc. 12 mo.*	*Act. over budget*	*Act. under budget*	*Summary*
Rent	$14.00	$168.00	$168.00	$727.87			
Food	28.84	346.08	337.90			$ 8.18	
F. & L.	3.25	39.00	40.97		$ 1.97		
Clo.	10.00	120.00	70.43			49.57	Bal. end
Sund.	4.40	52.80	106.92		54.12		of 12 mo.
C. F.			2.70		2.70		$.95
	$60.49	$725.88	$726.92	$727.87	$58.79	$57.75	

	Est. of needs 1 mo.	*12 mo.*	*Act. Exp. 12 mo.*	*Act. Inc. 12 mo.*	*Act. over budget*	*Act. under budget*	*Summary*
Family No. 56, Woman, 5 children, 17, 15, 11, 9, 7							
Rent	$15.00	$180.00	$174.50	$897.56		$ 5.50	
Food	38.50	502.00	370.01			131.99	
F. & L.	3.25	39.00	54.62		$15.62		
Clo.	12.00	144.00	109.14			34.86	
Sund	2.44	29.28	123.23		93.95		Bal. end
C. F.	2.60	31.20	58.50		27.30		of 12 mo.
Debt pd			3.31		3.31		$4.25
	$73.79	$925.43	$893.31	$897.46	$140.18	$172.35	
Family No. 57, Woman, 5 children, 13, 12, 9, 7, 5							
Rent	$18.00	$216.00	$216.00	$863.57			
Food	31.12	373.44	369.96			$ 3.48	
F. & L.	3.25	39.00	50.87		$11.87		Bal. end
Clo.	12.00	144.00	62.35			81.65	of 12 mo.
Sund	4.40	52.80	73.31		20.51		$91.08
	$68.77	$825.24	$772.49	$863.57	$32.38	$85.13	
Family No. 58, Woman, 5 children, 17, 15, 13, 7, 4							
Rent	$13.00	$156.00	$156.00	$845.97			
Food	33.58	402.96	411.73		$ 8.77		
F. & L.	3.25	39.00	29.23			$ 9.77	
Clo.	10.00	120.00	96.64			23.36	Bal. end
Sund	3.91	46.92	51.57		4.65		of 12 mo.
C. F.	2.40	28.80	82.60		53.80		$18.20
	$66.14	$793.68	$827.77	$845.97	$67.22	$33.13	
Family No. 59, Woman, 5 children, 10, 7, 4, 3, 18 months							
Rent	$14.00	$168.00	$176.00	$692.84	$ 8.00		
Food	25.27	303.24	316.49		13.25		
F. & L.	3.25	39.00	53.20		14.20		Bal. end
Clo.	12.00	144.00	76.84			$67.16	of 12 mo.
Sund	3.52	42.24	69.24		27.00		$1.07
	$58.04	$696.48	$691.77	$692.84	$62.45	$67.16	
Family No. 60, Woman, 5 children, 11, 10, 8, 5, 4							
Rent	$11.50	$138.00	$138.00	$685.81			
Food	30.94	371.28	347.42			$23.86	
F. & L.	3.25	39.00	47.55		$ 8.55		Bal. end
Clo.	12.00	144.00	124.05			19.95	of 12 mo.
Sund	2.00	24.00	29.32		5.32		$.53
	$59.69	$716.28	$686.34	$685.81	$13.87	$43.81	

Family No. 61, Woman, 5 children, 13, 11, 9, 8, 5

	Est. of needs 1 mo.	*12 mo.*	*Act. Exp. 12 mo.*	*Act. Inc. 12 mo.*	*Act. over budget*	*Act. under budget*	*Summary*
Rent	$16.00	$192.00	$176.00	$767.62		$16.00	
Food	31.26	375.12	383.90		$ 8.78		
F. & L.	3.25	39.00	36.68			2.32	
Clo.	12.00	144.00	74.06			69.94	Bal. end
Sund.	3.95	47.40	86.03		38.63		of 12 mo.
C. F.	5.20	62.40	8.75			53.65	$2.20
	$71.66	$859.92	$765.42	$767.62	$47.41	$141.91	

Family No. 62, Woman, 5 children, 13, 11, 8, 4, 2

	Est. of needs 1 mo.	*12 mo.*	*Act. Exp. 12 mo.*	*Act. Inc. 12 mo.*	*Act. over budget*	*Act. under budget*	*Summary*
Rent	$15.00	$180.00	$180.00	$764.43			
Food	30.00	360.00	380.39		$20.39		
F. & L.	3.25	39.00	35.00			$ 4.00	Bal. end
Clo.	14.00	168.00	129.79			38.21	of 12 mo.
Sund.	5.03	60.36	38.70			21.66	$.55
	$67.28	$807.36	$763.88	$764.43	$20.39	$63.87	

Family No. 63, Woman, 5 children, 11, 10, 8, 7, 4

	Est. of needs 1 mo.	*12 mo.*	*Act. Exp. 12 mo.*	*Act. Inc. 12 mo.*	*Act. over budget*	*Act. under budget*	*Summary*
Rent	$11.00	$132.00	$132.00	$681.98			
Food	30.94	371.28	360.24			$11.04	
F. & L.	3.25	39.00	19.43			19.57	Bal. end
Clo.	10.00	120.00	76.19			43.81	of 12 mo.
Sund.	4.40	52.30	89.72		$37.42		$4.40
	$59.59	$714.58	$677.58	$681.98	$37.42	$74.42	

Family No. 64, Woman, 6 children, 13, 11, 10, 7, 5, 8 mo.

	Est. of needs 1 mo.	*12 mo.*	*Act. Exp. 12 mo.*	*Act. Inc. 12 mo.*	*Act. over budget*	*Act. under budget*	*Summary*
Rent	$13.00	$156.00	$169.00	$767.98	$13.00		
Food	30.67	368.04	390.29		22.25		
F. & L.	3.25	39.00	40.20		1.20		Bal. end
Clo.	10.00	120.00	109.04			$10.96	of 12 mo.
Sund.	3.08	36.96	55.69		18.73		$3.76
	$60.00	$720.00	$764.22	$767.98	$55.18	$10.96	

Family No. 65, Woman, 6 children, 14, 13, 10, 9, 7, 6

	Est. of needs 1 mo.	*12 mo.*	*Act. Exp. 12 mo.*	*Act. Inc. 12 mo.*	*Act. over budget*	*Act. under budget*	*Summary*
Rent	$14.00	$168.00	$168.00	$851.76			
Food	37.67	442.04	431.13			$10.91	
F. & L.	3.25	39.00	44.03		$ 5.03		Bal. end
Clo.	14.00	168.00	124.76			43.24	of 12 mo.
Sund.	7.70	92.40	72.77			19.63	$11.07
	$76.62	$909.44	$840.69	$851.76	$ 5.03	$73.78	

	Est. of needs *1 mo.*	*12 mo.*	*Act. Exp.* *12 mo.*	*Act. Inc.* *12 mo.*	*Act. over budget*	*Act. under budget*	*Summary*
Family No. 66, Woman, 6 children, 16, 14, 12, 10, 8, 5							
Rent	$12.00	$144.00	$125.00	$913.15		$19.00	
Food	38.95	467.40	521.88		$54.48		
F. & L.	3.25	39.00	17.19			21.81	
Clo.	12.00	144.00	83.96			60.04	Bal. end
Sund.	5.18	62.16	84.91		22.75		of 12 mo.
C. F.	5.20	62.40	74.15		11.75		$6.06
	$76.58	$918.96	$907.09	$913.15	$88.23	$100.85	
Family No. 67, Woman, 6 children, 19, 18, 15, 14, 9, 6							
Rent	$18.00	$216.00	$243.00	$1,172.50	$27.00		
Food	40.13	481.56	561.74		80.18		
F. & L.	3.25	39.00	63.82		24.82		
Clo.	12.00	144.00	91.67			$52.33	Bal. end
Sund.	2.00	24.00	173.67		149.67		of 12 mo.
C. F.			30.80		30.80		$7.80
	$75.38	$904.56	$1,164.70	$1,172.50	$312.47	$52.33	
Family No. 68, Woman, 6 children, 16, 13, 11, 8, 6, 2							
Rent	$15.00	$180.00	$ 81.00	$417.25		$99.00	
Food	28.67	344.04	178.33			165.71	
F. & L.	3.25	39.00	15.73			23.27	Bal. end
Clo.	10.00	120.00	80.33			39.67	of 12 mo.
Sund.	2.00	24.00	51.27		$27.27		$10.59
	$58.92	$707.04	$406.66	$417.25	$27.27	$327.65	
Family No. 69, Woman, 6 children, 15, 13, 9, 7, 6, 4							
Rent	$15.00	$180.00	$175.00	$790.31		$ 5.00	
Food	28.67	344.04	388.61		$44.57		
F. & L.	3.25	39.00	42.72		3.72		Bal. end
Clo.	12.00	144.00	36.80			107.20	of 12 mo.
Sund.	4.60	55.20	89.78		34.58		$29.33
	$63.52	$762.24	$732.91	$790.31	$82.87	$112.20	
Family No. 70, Woman, 7 children, 15, 14, 12, 11, 10, 6, 5							
Rent	$12.50	$150.00	$153.00	$765.88	$ 3.00		
Food	37.67	452.04	362.99			$89.05	
F. & L.	3.25	39.00	57.14		18.14		Bal. end
Clo.	14.00	168.00	61.27			106.73	of 12 mo.
Sund.	62.65	91.80	99.22		7.42		$32.26
	$70.07	$900.84	$733.62	$765.88	$28.56	195.78	

	Est. of needs 1 mo.	*12 mo.*	*Act. Exp. 12 mo.*	*Act. Inc. 12 mo.*	*Act. over budget*	*Act. under budget*	*Summary*
Family No. 71, Woman, 7 children, 17, 15, 13, 11, 9, 7, 3							
Rent	$20.00	$240.00	$203.00	$1,139.32		$37.00	
Food	45.86	550.32	520.88			29.44	
F. & L.	3.25	39.00	42.44		$ 3.44		
Clo.	16.00	192.00	163.43			28.57	Bal. end
Sund.	2.84	34.08	109.66		75.58		of 12 mo.
C. F.	15.60	187.20	94.39			92.81	$5.52
	$103.55	$1,242.60	$1,133.80	$1,139.32	$79.02	$187.82	
Family No. 72, Woman, 7 children, 16, 14, 11, 9, 7, 4, 2							
Rent	$14.00	$168.00	$168.00	$852.17			
Food	40.95	491.40	410.35			$81.05	
F. & L.	3.25	39.00	30.00			9.00	
Clo.	12.00	144.00	115.87			28.13	Bal. end
Sund.	4.38	52.56	63.98		$11.42		of 12 mo.
C. F.	5.20	62.40	53.55			8.85	$10.42
	$79.78	$957.36	$841.75	$852.17	$11.42	$127.03	
Family No. 73, Woman, 7 children, 15, 14, 12, 10, 9, 7, 4							
Rent	$15.00	$180.00	$132.00	$898.68		$48.00	
Food	36.04	432.48	449.81		$17.33		
F. & L.	3.25	39.00	65.61		26.61		
Clo.	14.00	168.00	64.93			103.07	Bal end.
Sund.	3.64	43.68	174.42		130.74		of 12 mo.
C. F.	2.60	31.20	9.60			21.60	$2.31
	$74.53	$894.36	$896.37	$898.68	$174.68	$172.67	
Family No. 74, Woman, 7 children, 18, 16, 14, 12, 8, 7, 5							
Rent	$17.00	$204.00	$198.00	$1,145.41		$ 6.00	
Food	46.68	560.16	626.67		$66.51		
F. & L.	3.25	39.00	40.13		1.13		Bal. end
Clo.	16.00	192.00	111.68			80.32	of 12 mo.
Sund.	5.00	60.00	170.86		110.86		$1.93
	$87.93	$1,055.16	$1,147.34	$1,145.41	$178.50	$86.32	
Family No. 75, Woman, 8 children, 17, 15, 13, 10, 9, 8, 7, 5							
Rent	$15.50	$186.00	$161.00	$930.00		$25.00	
Food	49.14	589.68	502.55			87.13	
F. & L.	3.25	39.00	31.96			7.04	Bal. end
Clo.	18.00	216.00	91.77			124.23	of 12 mo.
Sund.	5.54	66.48	135.36		$68.88		$7.36
	$91.43	$1,097.16	$922.64	$930.00	$68.88	$243.40	

PART III

WHAT THE STUDY REVEALED

CHAPTER I

CONDITIONS PREVIOUS TO STEADY INCOME

THE families have been known to the Association for varying periods before the death of the breadwinner. In all cases the income had been irregular or insufficient or both for a considerable time. The health of various members had suffered accordingly.

Before the granting of the regular income there was careful instruction in each family for at least six months. During this time members of the Home Economics' staff gave lessons in planning, buying and feeding, so that the housekeeper might be prepared to use her income to the best advantage.

During the time when the various families were being supported by the mothers' earnings, by church and other societies, the income was indeterminate in fifty-nine of the families. In the other sixteen it was possible to approximate the income. Of this number, according to the estimate on which this study is based, there was a deficit in all cases, the highest being $34.00 per month, the lowest $1.00, and the average $14.00 monthly. It is safe to say that not one of the seventy-five families had escaped some degree of ill health because of insufficient income.

After the allowances were granted the families were grouped according to income as follows:

Income	*Number of Families*
Between 200 and 300	1
" 300 " 400	2
" 400 " 500	8
" 500 " 600	22
" 600 " 700	18
" 700 " 800	12
" 800 " 900	7
" 900 " 1000	2
" 1100 " 1200	3
	75

At the end of the first year of steady income six of the seventy-five showed a deficit, the average deficit for the twelve months being $27.99. The remaining sixty-nine showed a surplus, the average being $9.72.

The following table shows the number of families who spent more than the estimate, and the average amount of this expenditure, also the number of families who spent less than the estimate of the average sum in each case:

ITEMIZED ANALYSIS OF THE ABOVE

Item	*No. Families Above*	*Average Sum*	*No. Families Below*	*Average Sum*
Rent	18	$14.97	31	$18.02
Food	38	29.80	37	29.30
Fuel and Light	24	8.12	51	11.30
Clothing	5	15.43	70	54.55
Insurance*	29	12.43	32	4.92
Sundries	64	28.35	11	10.94
Carfare	8	28.37	6	35.30

One important part of the plan was the supervision of health conditions by the Association's nurses. Before the granting of the cash allowance a record was made of the health of each member of all the families after a careful medical examination. The nurses' records show the progress from month to month, and the following is a verbatim report of conditions in each family at the end of the year:

HEALTH CONDITIONS AFTER A YEAR OF STEADY INCOME

Family	*Health After Year of Teaching and Steady Income*
Family No. 1	Family well.
" " 2	Conditions satisfactory.

* Budgets include insurance under Sundries.

Family	*Health After Year of Teaching and Steady Income*
Family No. 3	Children improved in health.
" " 4	Health of family improved.
" " 5	Family all well.
" " 6	Plan a success. Conditions excellent.
" " 7	Children improved. Medical care given. Satisfactory results.
" " 8	Conditions satisfactory.
" " 9	Health good.
" " 10	Family all in better health.
" " 11	Marked difference in health.
" " 12	Health improved. Steady advance at all points.
" " 13	Health of family good.
" " 14	Family all in better health.
" " 15	Children show good effects from care from mother.
" " 16	Good results.
" " 17	Improved in all ways.
" " 18	General health of family good.
" " 19	Excellent health.
" " 20	Woman and children all show marked improvement.
" " 21	Entire family well.
" " 22	Woman delicate but improved in health. Children well.
" " 23	Conditions much improved. Health of family good.
" " 24	Health of all the family improved.
" " 25	Children show good effects of home care of mother. Health improved.
" " 26	Children well. Woman much improved.
" " 27	Living conditions greatly improved. Woman under medical care.
" " 28	Health conditions satisfactory.
" " 29	Health of family good.
" " 30	Health much improved.
" " 31	Health good.

Family	*Health After Year of Teaching and Steady Income*
Family No. 32	All the family well.
" " 33	All the family show marked improvement in health since steady income.
" " 34	Woman not strong but great improvement noted in all members of the family.
" " 35	Slow but steady improvement.
" " 36	Family all well.
" " 37	Health decidedly improved.
" " 38	Great improvement in health.
" " 39	Family better but still shows the effect of long continued under-nourishment.
" " 40	Family greatly improved since granting of steady income.
" " 41	Great improvement in health of all the family.
" " 42	Health of family good.
" " 43	Slow but steady improvement.
" " 44	Health of family good.
" " 45	Health decidedly improved.
" " 46	Woman's health improving rapidly after steady income came.
" " 47	Steady improvement in every possible way.
" " 48	Much better health.
" " 49	Family well.
" " 50	Health improved but still below.
" " 51	General health of all the family good.
" " 52	Woman and children all well.
" " 53	Family in good health.
" " 54	Entire family well.
" " 55	Health of entire family improved since steady income began.
" " 56	Remarkable gain in health of all members of the family.
" " 57	Family improved rapidly.
" " 58	Remarkable improvement.
" " 59	Steady improvement.
" " 60	Good improvement in all the family.

Family	*Health After Year of Teaching and Steady Income*
Family No. 61	Woman gaining strength and courage.
" " 62	Vast improvement in all directions.
" " 63	Steadily improving.
" " 64	Steady improvement. Children very well.
" " 65	All conditions improving rapidly.
" " 66	Children show splendid improvement.
" " 67	All improved.
" " 68	Entire family well.
" " 69	Family all improved.
" " 70	All well.
" " 71	Slow but steady improvement.
" " 72	Excellent health.
" " 73	Family all well.
" " 74	Conditions improved.
" " 75	Steady improvement.

The most cursory examination of the above records leads inevitably to the conclusion that even a minimum sum carefully administered, will do much for families who have been living on a "hand-to-mouth" basis.

We may sum up as follows: A carefully planned minimum standard can lay the foundation of good health for all members of the family. Such a sum can restore shattered nerves and renew courage for a mother who has been harassed by irregular and uncertain payments of an income inadequate at the best. Such an assured minimum can change pale and listless children into rosy-cheeked romping boys and girls.

It is worth while to consider now just what practical application can be made of the facts noted above. The present study is not concerned primarily with the sources of the family income. This income may be received in the form of a pension from private or State funds, from the earnings of the children, or from the combined earnings of all the members of the family. One object has been to help in fixing an adequate standard of living for families in corresponding income groups.

In the succeeding pages when the items of the estimate are discussed in detail there will be suggestions for improvement in this estimate. These suggestions may lead it is hoped to the consideration of the next step in this campaign of home preservation. This next step will be to discuss just how much must be added to the estimate of living needs so that the family income may provide a comfortable balance.

CHAPTER II

Housing Conditions

The sum paid for rent was largely a concession to circumstances. It will be worth while to ascertain, first, the percentage spent for rent by each family according to income; second, the number of rooms needed to keep the family in health and comfort; third, the maximum of convenience procurable by families in this income group; and finally, the fluctuations of rent according to the number of rooms.

Of the seventy-five families, one with an income of \$200–\$300, paid its rent by janitor service; families in the \$300–\$400 group paid 28% of their income for rent; those in the \$400–\$500, a percentage of 17–25; in the \$500–\$600, a percentage of 16–33; in the \$600–\$700, a percentage of 18–38; in the \$700–\$800, a percentage of 18–34; in the \$800–\$900, a percentage of 16–33; in the \$900–\$1,000, a percentage of 13–17; and in the \$1,000 to \$1,100 group, a percentage of 17–18 of the income.

NUMBER OF ROOMS NEEDED

Perhaps the best way to discuss this question is to give a report of the number of rooms the families actually had. It has already been stated that the housing conditions were somewhat of a compromise, and the workers were agreed that, while the families were comfortable in these quarters, and while the rent paid was all that they could afford, ideally, 50% of the families should have had at least one room additional.

When considered according to the number of rooms needed, the families fall into the following groups:

Group 1—three families of three individuals each, one of these having three rooms, the other two families having four rooms.

Group 2—twenty-six families of four individuals, one having two rooms, twelve having three rooms, twelve having four rooms, and one having five rooms.

Group 3—nineteen families of five individuals each, seven having three rooms, ten having four rooms, and two having five rooms.

Group 4—fifteen families of six individuals

each, five having three rooms, eight having four rooms, and two having five rooms.

Group 5—six families of seven individuals each, three having three rooms, two having four rooms, and one having five rooms.

Group 6—five families of eight individuals each, four having four rooms, and one having five rooms.

Group 7—one family of nine individuals having four rooms.

CONVENIENCES

Of the seventy-five families, thirteen had private bathrooms, forty-four private toilets, thirty had joint use of toilets in the hall, and one, a toilet in the yard.

RENT ACCORDING TO NUMBER OF ROOMS

When considered according to the amount of space furnished for a given sum, the apartments may be grouped as follows:

Group 1—two apartments of two rooms, rent for each $10.00.

Group 2—twenty-nine apartments of three rooms; two having rent paid by janitor service, one renting at $7.50 per month, two at $8.00, one at $9.50, five at $10.00, four at $11.00, two at $12.00, eight at $13.00, two at $14.00, one at $15.00, and one at $19.00.

Group 3—forty apartments of four rooms; three of these having rent paid by janitor service, one at $10.50 per month, two at $11.00, three at $11.50, three at $12.00, seven at $13.00, one at $13.50, six at $14.00, three at $15.00, one at $15.50, two at $16.00, two at $17.00, two at $18.00, two at $20.00, and two at $21.00.

Group 4—six apartments of five rooms; one having rent paid by janitor service, one at $12.00 per month, one at $12.50, one at $14.00, one at $15.00, and one at $16.00 per month.

Examination of the expense accounts shows that none of the families can afford for rent a sum sufficient to insure really satisfactory housing. Indeed, one might say that existence in a typical tenement house is never wholly satisfactory from the point of view of sanitation, privacy and enjoyment. That our families live in them such well-ordered lives, is a tribute to the resourcefulness and pluck of the housekeeper, as well as to the general cheerfulness of spirit prevailing among the various members of the family group.

CHAPTER III

The Seventy-five Dietaries Considered in Detail

In fixing the ration allowance, the families are grouped according to size. It has already been stated that the ration allowance is planned so that groups of families may use it as a guide.

In the first group we have families numbers 1 to 29, inclusive, in the second group, families numbers 30 to 48, inclusive, in the third group, families numbers 49 to 69, inclusive, in the fifth group, families numbers 70 to 74, inclusive, and family number 75, forms the sixth group.

THE SEVENTY-FIVE DIETARIES IN DETAIL

Group 1

Food Allowance		*Food Purchased by Families* Family No. 1	No. 2	No. 3	No. 4	No. 5	No. 6	No. 7
Bread, cake, pastry	416 lbs.	1612 lbs.	747 lbs.	613 lbs.	947 lbs.	561 lbs.	1330 lbs.	582 lbs.
Butter and other fats.......	78 "	31 "	10 "	29 "	30 "	78 "	53 "	47 "
Milk.....................	730 qts.	348 qts.	619 qts	291 qts.	600 qts.	284 qts.	512 qts.	350 qts.
Meat, eggs, fish............	169 lbs.	360 lbs.	311 lbs.	220 lbs.	300 lbs.	254 lbs.	266 lbs.	298 lbs.
Fruit and vegetables.......	909 "	928 "	944 "	729 "	1734 "	761 "	1401 "	962 "
Cereal....................	156 "	309 "	178 "	154 "	668 "	162 "	222 "	143 "
Sugar....................	169 "	78 "	124 "	152 "	174 "	61 "	76 "	72 "
Potatoes.................	519 "	389 "	304 "	413 "	431 "	178 "	238 "	194 "

		Family No. 8	No. 9	No. 10	No. 11	No. 12	No. 13	No. 14
Bread, cake, pastry........	416 lbs.	1560 lbs.	996 lbs.	535 lbs.	1141 lbs.	1308 lbs.	1465 lbs.	933 lbs.
Butter and other fats.......	78 "	81 "	31 "	54 "	51 "	31 "	54 "	46 "
Milk.....................	730 qts.	502 qts.	678 qts.	728 qts	726 qts.	788 qts.	651 qts.	216 qts.
Meat, eggs, fish............	169 lbs.	355 lbs.	286 lbs.	259 lbs.	156 lbs.	379 lbs.	491 lbs.	359 lbs.
Fruit and vegetables.......	909 "	704 "	722 "	1230 "	472 "	1142 "	1119 "	1066 "
Cereal....................	156 "	161 "	168 "	206 "	170 "	244 "	180 "	213 "
Sugar....................	169 "	122 "	77 "	108 "	110 "	124 "	182 "	100 "
Potatoes.................	519 "	304 "	314 "	405 "	222 "	318 "	180 "	542 "

Group 1—*Continued*

Food Allowance		Food Purchased by Families: Family No. 15	No. 16	No. 17	No. 18	No. 19	No. 20	No. 21	No. 22
Bread, cake, pastry	416 lbs.	1268 lbs.	1250 lbs.	1766 lbs.	685 lbs.	1659 lbs.	884 lbs.	955 lbs.	1547 lbs.
Butter and other fats	78 "	31 "	38 "	33 "	40 "	46 "	49 "	30 "	30 "
Milk	730 qts.	807 qts.	532 qts.	668 qts.	504 qts.	495 qts.	622 qts.	353 qts.	141 qts.
Meat, eggs, fish	169 lbs.	302 lbs.	330 lbs.	317 lbs.	272 lbs.	234 lbs.	303 lbs.	377 lbs.	88 lbs.
Fruit and vegetables	909 "	1143 "	947 "	686 "	1284 "	1013 "	3615 "	1225 "	13 "
Cereal	156 "	350 "	223 "	102 "	204 "	212 "	53 "	234 "	281 "
Sugar	169 "	114 "	109 "	167 "	29 "	85 "	96 "	94 "	102 "
Potatoes	519 "	284 "	365 "	208 "	278 "	248 "	305 "	246 "	265 "

Food Allowance		Family No. 23	No. 24	No. 25	No. 26	No. 27	No. 28	No. 29	*Average*
Bread, cake, pastry	416 lbs.	1737 lbs.	1382 lbs.	1630 lbs.	1177 lbs.	1052 lbs.	329 lbs.	669 lbs.	1114
Butter and other fats	78 "	35 "	31 "	62 "	31 "	34 "	43 "	54 "	48
Milk	730 qts.	774 qts.	300 qts.	537 qts.	594 qts.	604 qts.	681 qts.	708 qts.	538
Meat, eggs, fish	169 lbs.	256 lbs.	263 lbs.	360 lbs.	309 lbs.	121 lbs.	227 lbs.	310 lbs.	369
Fruit and vegetables	909 "	922 "	859 "	733 "	640 "	886 "	1638 "	788 "	1045
Cereal	156 "	71 "	340 "	139 "	237 "	213 "	122 "	255 "	214
Sugar	169 "	131 "	78 "	113 "	65 "	66 "	51 "	126 "	102
Potatoes	519 "	363 "	338 "	322 "	274 "	292 "	186 "	271 "	519

GROUP 2

Food Allowance		*Food Purchased by Families* Family No. 30	No. 31	No. 32	No. 33	No. 34	No. 35
Bread, cake, pastry	473 lbs.	2223 lbs.	1078 lbs.	948 lbs.	1661 lbs.	1029 lbs.	359 lbs.
Butter and other fats	78 "	51 "	25 "	22 "	81 "	56 "	51 "
Milk	728 qts.	710 qts.	519 qts.	365 qts.	728 qts.	374 qts.	756 qts.
Meat, eggs, fish	208 lbs.	83 lbs.	302 lbs.	203 lbs.	476 lbs.	445 lbs.	480 lbs.
Fruit and vegetables	935 "	1217 "	538 "	837 "	1722 "	1070 "	1277 "
Cereal	208 "	236 "	165 "	117 "	473 "	282 "	247 "
Sugar	182 "	152 "	81 "	52 "	205 "	113 "	124 "
Potatoes	624 "	343 "	430 "	340 "	567 "	578 "	276 "

		Family No. 36	No. 37	No. 38	No. 39	No. 40	No. 41	No. 42
Bread, cake, pastry	473 lbs.	1031 lbs.	691 lbs.	1014 lbs.	1309 lbs.	1600 lbs.	745 lbs.	1364 lbs.
Butter and other fats	78 "	32 "	41 "	27 "	33 "	28 "	55 "	81 "
Milk	730 qts.	503 qts.	776 qts.	600 qts.	657 qts.	340 qts.	14 qts.	559 qts.
Meat, eggs, fish	208 lbs.	321 lbs.	244 lbs.	407 lbs.	455 lbs.	405 lbs.	127 lbs.	376 lbs.
Fruit and vegetables	935 "	1050 "	917 "	987 "	778 "	2146 "	626 "	874 "
Cereal	208 "	183 "	152 "	160 "	137 "	83 "	121 "	264 "
Sugar	182 "	95 "	107 "	77 "	87 "	100 "	79 "	117 "
Potatoes	624 "	252 "	197 "	317 "	312 "	146 "	352 "	475 "

Group 2—*Continued*

Food Allowance		*Food Purchased by Families*						
		Family No. 43	No. 44	No. 45	No. 46	No. 47	No. 48	*Average*
Bread, cake, pastry	473 lbs.	1168 lbs.	1813 lbs.	1236 lbs.	1263 lbs.	1965 lbs.	770 lbs.	1225
Butter and other fats	78 "	64 "	46 "	30 "	28 "	9 "	40 "	42
Milk	730 qts.	731 qts.	481 qts.	626 qts.	702 qts.	272 qts.	600 qts.	542
Meat, eggs, fish	208 lbs.	334 lbs.	23 lbs.	554 lbs.	363 lbs.	480 lbs.	339 lbs.	337
Fruit and vegetables	935 "	1140 "	942 "	654 "	1543 "	915 "	1050 "	1057
Cereal	208 "	494 "	150 "	158 "	246 "	80 "	368 "	216
Sugar	182 "	127 "	100 "	95 "	114 "	2 "	98 "	101
Potatoes	624 "	292 "	263 "	301 "	278 "	573 "	440 "	354

Group 3

Food Allowance		*Food Purchased by Families*							
		Family No. 49	No. 50	No. 51	No. 52	No. 53	No. 54	No. 55	No. 56
Bread, cake, pastry	624 lbs.	1594 lbs.	1569 lbs.	1235 lbs.	1603 lbs.	1208 lbs.	1419 lbs.	951 lbs.	1306 lbs.
Butter and other fats	78 "	40 "	65 "	62 "	63 "	54 "	46 "	42 "	42 "
Milk	730 qts.	932 qts.	588 qts.	485 qts.	852 qts.	198 qts.	639 qts.	319 qts.	639 qts.
Meat, eggs, fish	266 lbs.	345 lbs.	247 lbs.	297 lbs.	352 lbs.	553 lbs.	329 lbs.	1018 lbs.	351 lbs.
Fruit and vegetables	935 "	795 "	836 "	668 "	607 "	937 "	683 "	731 "	1306 "
Cereal	260 "	416 "	404 "	306 "	383 "	154 "	317 "	148 "	285 "
Sugar	182 "	111 "	103 "	120 "	113 "	94 "	114 "	131 "	146 "
Potatoes	780 "	272 "	308 "	161 "	237 "	300 "	267 "	343 "	358 "

GROUP 3—*Continued*

Food Allowance		Family No. 57	No. 58	No. 59	No. 60	No. 61	No. 62	No. 63	*Average*
		Food Purchased by Families							
Bread, cake, pastry	624 lbs.	669 lbs.	957 lbs.	1076 lbs.	1222 lbs.	1958 lbs.	1219 lbs	1784 lbs.	1318
Butter and other fats	78 "	54 "	70 "	67 "	57 "	100 "	150 "	170 "	75
Milk	730 qts.	708 qts.	578 qts.	218 qts.	713 qts.	509 qts.	971 qts.	723 qts.	604
Meat, eggs, fish	266 lbs.	310 lbs.	445 lbs.	369 lbs.	419 lbs.	429 lbs.	424 lbs.	388 lbs.	331
Fruit and vegetables	935 "	788 "	1503 "	964 "	1620 "	1046 "	1316 "	667 "	957
Cereal	260 "	255 "	270 "	205 "	604 "	337 "	230 "	250 "	304
Sugar	182 "	126 "	121 "	75 "	134 "	114 "	194 "	115 "	169
Potatoes	780 "	271 "	773 "	525 "	453 "	514 "	430 "	541 "	519

GROUP 4

Food Allowance		Family No. 64	No. 65	No. 66	No. 67	No. 68	No. 69	*Average*
		Food Purchased by Families						
Bread, cake, pastry	754 lbs.	588 lbs	2517 lbs.	992 lbs.	1137 lbs.	1143 lbs.	1440 lbs.	1636
Butter and other fats	104 "	60 "	108 "	38 "	123 "	25 "	66 "	70
Milk	1091 qts.	836 qts.	1177 qts.	247 qts.	677 qts.	192 qts.	524 qts.	608
Meat, eggs, fish	208 lbs.	237 lbs.	472 lbs.	426 lbs.	823 lbs.	150 lbs.	561 lbs.	444
Fruit and vegetables	1351 "	1348 "	1366 "	1164 "	3159 "	500 "	342 "	1316
Cereal	312 "	326 "	301 "	121 "	160 "	204 "	2211 "	553
Sugar	247 "	122 "	270 "	112 "	1142 "	63 "	142 "	308
Potatoes	831 "	282 "	771 "	319 "	633 "	181 "	1045 "	538

GROUP 5

Food Allowance		Family No. 70	No. 71	No. 72	No. 73	No. 74	*Average*
		Food Purchased by Families					
Bread, cake, pastry	884 lbs.	1642 lbs.	3118 lbs.	1366 lbs.	1549 lbs.	3500 lbs.	2235
Butter and other fats	104 "	123 "	104 "	110 "	65 "	95 "	90
Milk	1091 qts.	550 qts.	1155 qts.	831 qts.	826 qts.	1012 qts.	874
Meat, eggs, fish	273 lbs.	394 lbs.	627 lbs.	312 lbs.	425 lbs.	616 lbs.	478
Fruit and vegetables	1715 "	871 "	1627 "	1442 "	2097 "	2376 "	1682
Cereal	338 "	233 "	474 "	340 "	119 "	902 "	413
Sugar	299 "	162 "	221 "	127 "	121 "	307 "	187
Potatoes	935 "	588 "	510 "	1179 "	498 "	572 "	669

GROUP 6

Food Allowance		Food Purchased by Families No. 75
Bread, cake, pastry	1179 lbs.	2023 lbs.
Butter and other fats	130 "	40 "
Milk	1091 qts.	744 qts.
Meat, eggs, fish	325 lbs.	365 lbs
Fruit and vegetables	1975 "	1617 "
Cereal	338 "	767 "
Sugar	351 "	151 "
Potatoes	1091 "	252 "

When the matter of instruction in diet was first contemplated the workers realized that they were facing a long campaign. In planning this campaign, the dietitians weighed carefully the need for each reform in diet, and the relative chances of success. They realized that it was a delicate matter to lay even the friendliest of hands on home matters, and so they decided to concentrate on one point at a time. Furthermore, it was planned to make each of these points the maximum of interest until some definite result should be accomplished. Left to its own devices, the average family in such a group, breakfasts on bread or sugar buns and tea. The noon meal, if "supper" is the chief one of the day, will probably be "something quick," mayhap potato-salad or ham from the delicatessen store, with more tea; while the hot supper, if there has been no interruption of pay day, will always have meat, and almost always the meat will be fried. Besides this there will be potatoes and sometimes a vegetable, with bread and coffee. "The children must take what we do"—this means the strong coffee and tea, cold lunches, fried food, with no certainty of the much needed milk, vegetables and fruit.

In judging results of the food work, each part of the plan of instruction will be considered separately. Besides this, the dietary standard as a whole, will be discussed in relation to what actually happened in the families.

The plan of instruction included the following:

1. Food value of milk and economy in its use.

2. The advantage of a reasonable amount of meat.

3. The necessity for fruits and vegetables.

4. The use of cereals to give variety to the starchy foods.

5. Harmful effects of tea and coffee for children.

We have already noted that the dietary standard was used merely as a guide. The families were given advice and instruction in food matters, but the final choice was left to each housekeeper. It was thought wisest to follow this course, since arbitrary dictation would defeat the chief aim of the instruction. Furthermore, the real value of the standard itself could be better judged if a reasonable amount of freedom of choice were given.

Summary of the Food Figures

	Families approaching Standard	Below	Above
Milk	60%	40%	
Meat		4%	96%
Fruit and Vegetables	54%	6%	40%
Bread	8%		92%
Cereals	41%	8%	51%

RESULTS FOLLOWING INSTRUCTION IN THE FOOD VALUE OF MILK

The dietitians feel that the results here were fairly satisfactory. Slow and patient work is needed to bring about changes in food habits, and the women responded very well in this particular. It is true that many educational agencies throughout the city have contributed to a popular knowledge concerning the value of milk, so that the A. I. C. P. workers found instruction on this point comparatively easy.

In 1906, when the home teaching began, few families were using milk of any description with any degree of regularity, and it was quite exceptional to find one using bottled milk. At the present time it is safe to say that it is the exception to find a family that does not at least realize the value of bottled milk.

The dietitians did not lose heart over the 40% of the families who fell below the milk standard. In each home there are special problems, and circumstances often conspire to make progress slow.

It was difficult at first to convince the housekeepers that they could "afford" to buy a liberal quantity of milk. After they were convinced that milk not only contributed to the health of the family, but that it also was literally a cheap food, the battle was practically won.

RESULTS FOLLOWING INSTRUCTION IN THE MODERATE USE OF MEAT

From the beginning the workers realized that they could accomplish only one thing at a time. They realized that all of the families were buying meat in too large quantities. Education in the value of milk was, however, thought to be of primary importance, and the results of this are noted above.

The results of the meat instruction do not appear on the surface at first glance. The dietitians succeeded in reducing the excessive amount very considerably in nearly every family. Beside this, in fixing the food standard the workers realized that the meat item was so low that probably none of the families would follow it exactly. The teachers felt sure, however, that no real harm would come from the small proportion of meat, since the other foods were being shifted into their right relationships.

During the periods of irregular income preceding instruction, large purchases of meat were made whenever there was a temporary increase of money. The dietitians worked very hard to guard against such unwise planning in the future. Women were taught that it was harmful to the health of the families to let this item of food assume too large a place in the dietary.

RESULTS FOLLOWING INSTRUCTION IN USE OF FRUITS AND VEGETABLES

For some time one of the dietitian's difficulties had been to induce the families to use enough of these foods. It took much persuasion to convince mothers that oranges were anything but an extravagance. The merits of "plenty of milk and eggs" were extolled openly by the women, but the relation of carrots and spinach to bone material was quite a new idea. Because of these facts, and because of long acquaintance with the evils resulting from a diet low in fruit and vegetables, the dietitians were not unduly cast down over the fact that the pendulum swung too far the other way.

RESULTS FOLLOWING INSTRUCTION IN THE USE OF BREAD AND CEREALS

There is a tendency among many of the families of the hard working population to depend too largely on the diet of bread and tea. There are two reasons for this, first, its apparent cheapness, and second, the ease with which it can be served.

The dietitians realized this and from the beginning of the regular instruction kept these facts in mind. The plan was to introduce a variety of cereals and to cut down somewhat the expenditures for bread. A glance at the summary on page 69 shows that not much was accomplished along this line. It is true that a fair proportion came near the cereal allowance, but slightly more than half exceeded it and an overwhelming proportion went far beyond the bread allowance.

These facts raise some interesting questions in dietetics. During the time when the families were subsisting on a meagre diet it was not surprising that they craved the energy-giving qualities of starch as well as its bulk. Conditions during the present study were, however, quite different. There was an abundance of fruit and vegetables, and plenty of strength foods. The question seems to be how far shall this demand for breadstuffs be respected in formulating future dietary standards.

RESULTS FOLLOWING INSTRUCTION REGARDING TEA AND COFFEE

Figures showing actual purchases of tea and coffee have not been tabulated, since the effect of these articles on the actual dietary is indirect only. Instruction concerning the harmful effects of these beverages for children was continuous and results have been satisfactory. There is a close relationship in milk education and the decreased use of the tea and coffee. It was explained to the mothers that the use of these beverages tended to use up the strength of the children faster than the other foods could offset this evil of stimulations.

POINTS TO BE CONSIDERED IN THE FORMULATING OF A NEW RATION ALLOWANCE

1. It is probable that no change need be made in the quantity of milk advised.

2. The allowance of fruits and vegetables seems to be satisfactory.

3. Some work should be done on the question of fixing a standard amount of bread.

4. There should be a sufficiently liberal total allowance to permit the families some freedom in satisfying individual wants in the matter of flavor and variety.

CLASSIFICATION OF FOOD ACCORDING TO SIZE AND COMPOSITION OF FAMILY

Considering the food expenditure according to the size of families, we have the following groups:

Group 1—three families of three individuals each, one spending 46% of the income for food, one spending 71%, and one 74% of the income for food.

Group 2—twenty-six families of four individuals each, one spending 36% of the income for food, one 37%, one 38%, one 41%, two 43%, two 44%, three 45%, three 47%, three 48%, two 49%, three 50%, one 51%, one 52%, one 57%, and one 62% of the income for food.

Group 3—twenty families of five individuals each, one family spending 38% of the income for food, one 39%, one 40%, one 42%, one 44%, two 49%, three 50%, three 51%, two 52%, two 53%, one 54%, one 55%, and one 63% of the income for food.

Group 4—fifteen families of six individuals each, one spending 41% of the income for food, one 42%, one 45%, two 46%, two 47%, one 48%, two 49%, one 50%, one 52%, one 54%, and two 57%, of the income for food.

Group 5—six families of seven individuals each, one spending 42% of the income for food, one 47%, one 49%, two 50%, and one 57% of the income for food.

Group 6—four families of six individuals each, one spending 45% of the income for food, one 47%, one 48%, and one 50% of the income for food.

Group 7—one family of eight individuals spending 53% of the income for food.

It is a generally accepted fact that large families can buy to better advantage than small ones. In this group the advantage has not seemed to be so great as might have been expected. The percentage of expenditure for food remains surprisingly uniform.

CLASSIFICATION OF FOOD EXPENDITURES ACCORDING TO INCOME

Considered according to income the food expenditures of the families may be divided as follows:

Group 1—one family with an income of $200–$300 spending 71% of this income for food.

Group 2—two families with an income of $300–$400, one spending 48% for food, the other 74% of the income for food.

Group 3—nine families with an income of $400–$500, one spending 38% for food, one 42%, one 48%, one 52%, one 56%, two 57%, one 62%, and one 63% of the income for food.

Group 4—twenty-one families with an income of $500–$600, one spending 38% for food, one 41%, one 42%, one 43%, two 45%, one 46%, one 47%, one 48%, three 49%, three 50%, two 51%, two 52%, one 53%, and one 55%.

Group 5—eighteen families with an income of

$600–$700, one spending 36% for food, one 37%, one 39%, one 40%, two 44%, one 45%, two 47%, one 48%, one 49%, three 50%, one 51%, one 52%, one 53%, and one 54% of the income for food.

Group 6—twelve families with an income of $700–$800, one spending 43% for food, two 44%, one 45%, two 46%, one 47%, three 49%, one 50%, and one 53% of the income for food.

Group 7—seven families with an income of $800–$900, one spending 34% for food, one 41%, one 42%, two 48%, and two 50% of the income for food.

Group 8—two families with an income of $900–$1,000, one spending 53% and one 57% of the income for food.

Group 9—three families with an income of $1,000–$1,200, one spending 45% for food, one 47% and one 54% of the income for food.

From the above it is evident that the income must go beyond the $1,200 amount before a reasonable decrease may be expected in the percentage spent for food.

CHAPTER IV

The Clothing Budget

The clothing item constitutes one of the most serious phases of the problem. The fact that necessity leads the housekeeper to plan first of all for the rent, second for the food, and third for incidentals, shifts the clothing expenditure into a secondary place.

Circumstances make the lives of our unskilled working folk a series of vicious circles. The very lack of provision for various necessities contributes to the low state of health that, in turn, decreases the power to earn more.

In the case of the clothing, even with careful planning, the sum left after rent, food, and incidentals have been paid for will barely clothe the working and school members of the family. The housekeeper herself must eke out with cast-off garments. Women frequently say—"I have not had a hat, or a coat"—as the case may be—"for ten years."

Clean, comfortable and suitable clothing for the

house mother would react favorably on the welfare of the entire family. The fact that many of our families depend on gifts is not an unmixed blessing. There is a natural shrinking from the wearing of clothing belonging to persons outside of the family circle, and this aversion should be respected.

The following figures are perhaps one of the most significant in the entire study. In no case was the sum spent for clothing sufficient to provide properly for all members of the family. Later we shall have occasion to speak of the connection of this fact with the meagre appropriation for incidentals. Reference to the clothing estimate, page 13 will show, that the provision made was at the best scanty. The fact that not one of our families even approached this sum gives much food for thought.

The percentage spent for clothing is so low in every case, irrespective of income, that it is not possible to do much in the way of making comparisons.

In classifying the clothing expenditures according to income, the families fall into the following groups:

Group 1—one family with an income of \$200–\$300 spending 21% of this income for clothing.

Group 2—two families with an income of $300–$400, one spending 7%, and one 8% of the income for clothing.

Group 3—eight families with an income of $400–$500, one spending 2%, one 3%, one 8%, one 11%, one 12%, two 13%, and one 18% of the income for clothing.

Group 4—twenty-two families with an income of $500–$600, one spending 5%, one 7%, six 8%, three 9%, four 11%, two 12%, one 14%, and one 16% of the income for clothing.

Group 5—eighteen families with an income of $600–$700, one spending 4%, one 8%, two 7%, one 9%, four 10%, one 11%, two 12%, one 13%, two 14%, and three 18% of the income for clothing.

Group 6—twelve families with an income of $700–$800, one spending 4%, two 6%, one 8%, two 9%, two 10%, two 14%, and two 16% of the income for clothing.

Group 7—seven families with an income of $800–$900, one spending 7%, one 11%, two 13%, two 14%, and one 15% of the income for clothing.

Group 8—two families with an income of $900–$1,000, each spending 9% of the income for clothing.

Group 9—three families with an income of \$1,000–\$1,200, one spending 7%, one 8%, and one 14% of the income for clothing.

In fixing the sum allowed in the estimate for clothing, there was no attempt to set a standard. The Association made itself responsible only for the sum required to meet actual living needs. It has already been stated that practically all of the families depended largely upon gifts of clothing. This fact is another reason for not depending upon the women's own expense accounts for help in setting a standard. Furthermore, it was not practical to secure completely itemized accounts of clothing expenditures from any of the women. A good beginning was made in this direction, however. Systematic record keeping was in itself a tax at first, and the workers made haste slowly here as in the case of the food work. Approximately only 50% of the clothing expenditure was fully itemized. The remaining items were entered in the account books simply as "clothing."

The entries for clothing that were itemized give details enough to furnish considerable help and information. For example, expenditures for both shoes and stockings were entered in detail in each case, as were those for "repairs." The following table is a fair average of the manner in which a clothing budget of $53.44 was spent. The family consisted of woman and three children, ten, nine and three years. The prices also give a good idea of those paid by all the families.

CLOTHING BUDGET

First Quarter

Shoes	$1.25	Shoes (2 pr.)	$ 3.00
Stockings, 1 pr.	.10	Underwear	.50
Apron	.20	Rompers	.25
Material	.35	Underwear	1.00
Collar	.10		
			$6.75

Second Quarter

Stockings, 2 pr.	.25	Rompers (2)	.50
Stockings, 3 pr.	.35	Kimonas (2)	.50
Stockings, 1 pr.	.10	Baby's hat	.10
Underwear	.50	Garters	.05
Boy's shoes	1.25	Stockings, 2 pr.	.25
2 dresses	.96	Dresses (2)	.98
Rompers	.25	Stockings, 2 pr.	.20
Stockings (3 pr.)	.30	Stockings, 2 pr.	.20
Child's dress	.49		
			$7.23

Third Quarter

Stockings, 1 pr.	$ .10	Underwear	.35
Stockings, 2 pr.	.20	Undervest	.19
Stockings, 3 pr.	.30	Rompers	.25
Stockings, 6 pr.	.60	Rompers	.25

Third Quarter—Continued

Dresses (2)	$ .98	Corsetcover	$ .15
Material	.30	Waist	.59
Gloves	.10	Shoes	1.50
Underwear	.49	Shoes, 2 pr.	3.50
Rubbers	.35	Repairs	.50
Rompers	.25	Ribbon	.20
Shoes	1.00	Hat	.49
Skirt	.25	Waist	.10
Ribbon	.10	Dress	.49
Rompers	.25		
Shirtwaist	.98		$14.81

Fourth Quarter

Repairs	$ .50	Stockings, 15 pr.	$1.50
Waist	.49	Rompers	.25
Dress	.49	Ribbon	.20
Underwear	.20	Shoes, 2 pr	2.50
Handkerchiefs	.15	Material	.25
Material	.50	Child's Shoes	.50
Repairs	1.50	Child's dress	.49
Shoes	1.25	Waist	.49
Underwear	.25	Repairs	.50
	$5.33		$6.68
			5.33
			$12.01

Itemized total for year	$40.80
Entered as "clothing"	12.64
Grand total	$53.44

The budget given is quoted verbatim from the housekeeper's own expense book and may be called typical of all the others.

It is probable that this housekeeper would have come very near to the estimated amount for clothing but for the fact that there was an unexpected falling off of $46.00 in the income of the family.

In commenting on the necessary educational work the sewing teacher of the Home Economics Division writes as follows: "The sum fixed in my estimate for clothing is not the ideal, but simply the best that can be done in the way of dividing a minimum income. The family clothing is usually sadly neglected—even the necessary things that are mentioned in the estimate are too often forgotten. The children are seldom provided with change of undergarments, and nightclothes are seldom thought of. I have tried to teach the mothers the necessity for these things, and to show them that to a limited extent even these can be purchased with the average income of the family in this group. In each family my instruction has included directions for keeping clean and self-respecting, as the result of thoughtful and careful buying."

In the foregoing paragraph Mrs. Ditmas touches on a vital part of the work. It is true that the comparative cheapness of ready-made garments must be considered. Experience and observation, however, lead to the conclusion that properly directed lessons in selection of fabrics and making of garments are necessary if the family problem is to be dealt with adequately.

Good results in nutrition depend directly on a budget that takes into consideration all the divisions of the family expenditures.

CHAPTER V

Fuel and Light

In comparing what actually happened with the "ideal division" spoken of on page 12 we realize that families living on a minimum basis can make only a very small provision for the item known as "operating expenses." In fact the mechanism of these households is so simple as to limit this item to the elemental ones of fuel and light. Study of the table on page 13 shows that very few of the families even approach the 8% of the income allowed in the "ideal division."

It has not been thought necessary to make tabulations as to the kinds of fuel used, since practically all of the families have at least a one-burner gas stove, and most of them, a coal range that may be used in very cold weather. During all except the most extreme weather, the housekeepers carefully save fuel, and the families become accustomed to unheated rooms.

One of the chief drawbacks in the tenement house life is the lack of provision for storage of even moderate amounts of either coal or wood. This makes it necessary for many of the housekeepers to buy coal "by the pail," and wood by the "bundle." This fact makes it impossible to estimate the fuel needs on an economical basis. The actual saving on fuel and light when purchased by the ton is 50%.

The expenditures for this item are surprisingly uniform. The average is for the entire group of Association families, approximately two thousand.

When grouped according to the percentage of income that was spent for fuel and light, the families may be classified thus:

Group 1—one family with an income of $200–$300, spending 10% of the income for fuel and light.

Group 2—two families with an income of $300–$400, one spending 7%, and one 4% of the income for fuel and light.

Group 3—eight families with an income of $400–$500, three spending 8%, one 4%, one 6%, one 7%, one 3%, one 10% of the income for fuel and light.

Group 4—twenty-two families with an income of $500–$600, three spending 5%, three 3%, three

7%, three 6%, six 4%, one 2%, and one 1% of the income for fuel and light.

Group 5—eighteen families with an income of $600–$700, six spending 5%, three 6%, three 2%, three 4%, one 8%, one 3%, and one 7% of the income for fuel and light.

Group 6—twelve families with an income of $700–$800, three spending 4%, five 5%, one 2%, one 3%, one 6%, and one 7% of the income for fuel and light.

Group 7—seven families with an income of $800–$900, two spending 5%, one 4%, one 6%, and three 7% of the income for fuel and light.

Group 8—two families with an income of $900–$1,000, one spending 5%, and one 7% of the income for fuel and light.

Group 9—three families with an income of $1,000–$1,200, two spending 3% and one 5% of the income for fuel and light.

CHAPTER VI

INCIDENTALS

WHEN considered according to the percentage of income spent for incidentals, the families fall into the following groups:

Group 1—one family with an income of $200–$300, spending 6% of the income for incidentals.

Group 2—two families with an income of $300–$400, one spending 7% and one 5% of the income for incidentals.

Group 3—eight families with an income of $400–$500, one spending 10%, one 9%, two 6%, two 4%, one 8%, and one 12% of the income for incidentals.

Group 4—twenty-two families with an income of $500–$600, four spending 9%, four 4%, one 7%, five 10%, three 6%, one 5%, two 8%, and two 3% of the income for incidentals.

Group 5—eighteen families with an income of $600–$700, one spending 18%, three 6%, four 9%, one 10%, one 11%, five 5%, one 3%, and two 8% of the income for incidentals.

Group 6—twelve families with an income of

$700–$800, one spending 12%, one 4%, two 6%, one 8%, three 9%, one 10%, two 5%, and one 7% of the income for incidentals.

Group 7—seven families with an income of $800–$900, one spending 14%, one 12%, two 4%, one 3%, one 17%, and one 8% of the income for incidentals.

Group 8—two families with an income of $900–$1,000, one spending 5%, and one 10% of the income for incidentals.

Group 9—three families with an income of $1,000–$1,200, one spending 9%, and two 8% of the income for incidentals.

As in the case of the clothing, it has been impossible to use the expense account as a standard on this point. This was due to the fact that the budgets were made out on a basis which allowed for no margin.

The expense books show several items common to all families. Church, household supplies, school supplies, laundry materials and insurance are the principal ones. Forty-seven of the seventy-five expense accounts showed entries for recreation, usually tickets for the movies. The average expenditure for recreation is $.30 a week.

The figures on page 51 will show how small a percentage of the income was available for incidentals. In families where large expenditures in this direction had to be made, the clothing item was invariably robbed.

A typical expense account for incidentals is given here:

ACTUAL EXPENDITURES FOR SUNDRIES

Family, 4 Individuals, $600–$700 Income

Laundry weekly (.22)	$11.44	Forward	$21.30
Church (.16)	8.32	Map for school	.10
Thread	.10	Pail	.16
Tooth powder	.10	Pictures	.20
Geography	.10	Table cloth	.59
Matches	.05	Joe's Club	.05
Shoe polish	.10	Stamps	.10
Needles	.05	Pictures	.20
Knife	.10	Paper	.10
Book	.04	Joe's Club	10
Shoe polish	.10	Joe's Club weekly	.05
Shoe polish	.10	Stamps	.10
Stamps	.08	Cards	.15
Papers	.06	Shelf paper	.10
Clothing hooks	.05	10 yds. sheeting	1.10
Stamps	.08	Towels	.66
Spending money	.03	Postals	.05
Pictures	.20	Towels	.15
Tooth paste	.10	Shoe polish	.08
Stamps	.08	Moving expenses	5.50
Thread	.02		
	$21.30		$30.84

Item	Amount	Item	Amount
Forward	$30.84	Forward	$36.54
Mattress	3.24	Matches	.05
Writing paper	.10	Postals	.07
Tooth paste	.10	Postals	.02
Paper	.07	Postals	.03
Writing paper	.10	Bell	.05
Pleasure	.40	Pictures	.40
Picture	.05	Stamps	.11
Darning cotton	.05	Writing paper	.15
Envelopes	.05	Embroidery	.16
School supplies	.10	Stamps	.04
Shoe polish	.10	Tooth paste	.10
Stove polish	.05	Matches	.05
Hair cut	.15	Refrigerator	2.00
Joe's Club	.05	Stamps	.04
Stamps	.02	Tooth paste	.10
Stamps	.10	Darning cotton	.05
Tea kettle	.45	Stamps	.04
1 pan	.37	Dues on book	.06
Spoon holder	.15	Shoe polish	.10
	$36.54	Total	$40.16

Perhaps no other one point as this of a small allowance for sundries shows so well what it means to any family to be without at least a moderate margin.

Families in the groups under discussion, those of the rank and file of wage earners, have much to give to our national life. The intensive work described in these pages has shown that it would be well worth while for neighborhoods and communities to undertake systematic coöperation for the purpose of building for future strength. Every family that learns to attain its potential best, physical, mental and spiritual, is a strong power. The problems of independent families are closely allied to those of the families under discussion. Conservation of all resources among independent families reduces to a minimum the number on the verge of the so-called poverty line.

Someone has said that the essential difference between poverty and riches is—"To be fifty dollars ahead, or fifty dollars behind." If this test were applied to our seventy-five families only three would be above the poverty line. If, however, we interpret the words "poverty" and "riches" in the larger sense, we might hope that all families in the group were richer at the end of the year than at the beginning—richer in understanding of their own needs, in formulating plans for meeting these needs, in the realization that each family had a place of its own to fill in the social scheme, and richer in courage to meet the task of preparing to fill this place.

Printed in the United States of America

BY THE SAME AUTHOR

Food for the Invalid and the Convalescent

$0.75

A great many books of special menus have been published, but upon one and all the same comment may be made—they are too elaborate. They mean either the expenditure of too much money or too much time and patience. It has long been realized that there was a decided need for a book of few pages which shall concisely set forth simple, inexpensive meals from which the greatest amount of nutritive values may be obtained.

This has been exactly Miss Winifred Stuart Gibbs's purpose in this work, a fitting sub-title for which might be "A Maximum of Nutrition, a Minimum of Expenditure." Beginning with a few general articles on how to buy food, how to keep food from spoiling, the kinds of food to eat, the necessity of good cooking and how to cook, Miss Gibbs passes rapidly to her two main considerations, the preparation of the various classes of food and the combinations of food into special menus and diets. In the first part, drinks, liquid foods, soups, meats, fats, fish, eggs, cereals, breads, vegetables, fruits and desserts are considered, while in the second part the menus are divided into three classes, those for the healthy, for children, and for the sick and convalescent.

www.ingramcontent.com/pod-product-compliance
Lightning Source LLC
LaVergne TN
LVHW021426110826
845150LV00007B/2099

* 9 7 8 1 4 2 5 5 0 9 0 0 2 *